THE SACRED PATH OF MIDWIFERY

by

Karen Melody Shatar, CNM

Llumina Press

Requests for permission to make copies of any part of this work should be mailed to Permissions Department, Llumina Press, PO Box 772246, Coral Springs, FL 33077-2246

ISBN: 1-932047-07-7

Printed in the United States of America

Birth is one of the most magical journeys into the Great Mystery that any woman ever undertakes in her lifetime. It is filled with endless possibilities. We learn to create a new dream out of a web formed from our own unique experience of living. We are challenged to come into our individual greatness. Our definition of the truth is questioned, the truth by which we live our lives, define our choices, and make our decisions. We become seekers, seekers of a sacred path, as a result of being thrust into the sacred space of the creative feminine aspect of our innermost being. Through this encounter we move into the essence of our being, and into a more truthful relatedness with our inner world and outer world alike.

DEDICATION:

To all of my family, friends, co-workers, fellow midwives, physicians, former clients and their families who have made it possible for me to embark upon this journey to find my own truth inside my own heart. Each of you knows who you are.

NAMASTE

The POWER of birthing

   Continues to show women who they are to themselves

      And to others . . .

      For we cannot give birth without also catching a glimpse

Of our SACRED reflections

   In the clear light of SPIRIT

TABLE OF CONTENTS

Birth is not something that happens to us . . .

It is something that emerges from deep within us . . .

And opens us to the MYSTERY . . .

Before the art of medicine comes the art of belief.

DEEPAK CHOPRA, MD

Prologue

Life continually unfolds to reveal the miraculous, each and every moment of our existence. There are great moments that stand out forever in our memories—falling in love, meeting a treasured friend after a long separation, giving birth, or saying a final goodbye to a loved one. And there are sweet simple moments—a quiet sunrise or stunning sunset that stills the breath and the heart, the sound and smell of a gentle rain, or a cool breeze that softly caresses.

It is in these precious moments that we begin to see that life is a timeless and eternal process of birthing. We give birth to new understandings, new hopes and dreams, heightened awareness, and new undertakings. We birth new challenges and new ways of being in the world, as well as giving birth to a new life. We each come to midwife ourselves in these processes and we learn to midwife each other as we support, encourage, and love those close to us.

I have had the good fortune of practicing as a nurse midwife during the past sixteen years. It is a path that has led me, sometimes gently and sometimes more urgently, sometimes painfully and sometimes joyfully, towards a sense of myself, and towards a state of wholeness and integrity, wisdom and compassion. It has led me to embrace life and its continuous process of transformation. My journey is far from complete, and yet the path itself has been one of the greatest blessings of my life. It is because of the blessings I have been given that I wish to write this book and offer these words in the spirit of thanksgiving.

It has been my experience that people are always fascinated and often in awe of this path of being with women in birth. It probes deeply into the magic and mystery of life and death; of the sacred and holy; of the honor of witnessing the power and beauty and holiness of the birth of an innocent, precious being. It touches a place of power and stillness within us that reveals us to ourselves in ways ordinary mirrors cannot. It puts us intensely and intimately in touch with extraordinary life. It is both incredibly magical and quite common.

In one sense, this is a book about the making of a midwife. In another, it is a book about my journey through life and about my relationships with the women and families I have encountered upon the way and how they have taught me and affected me. It is uniquely my story, dealing with my personal struggles and challenges and how I have learned and grown and changed and evolved. And yet I believe that it holds some universal ideas of what it means to be a midwife, both professionally and personally.

This book is written for those who find the sometimes simple and sometimes more complex journey of our lives fascinating, as well as for those who are intrigued by the process of birthing itself. It is written for those who would like to share what it is like to witness and participate daily in this magical unfolding of life's energy. This book is about the mystical connections we have with each other and about the Divine that guides and protects each of us as we dance the dance of life. It is about the ground of relatedness on which the spiritual and worldly paths meet and merge, continually pointing the way inward to what is holy and sacred and what rests in unity. It is essentially about our relationships–with a higher power, with ourselves, and with each other.

I have spent my entire adult career, over thirty years now, working with women in pregnancy and birth, and I have attended well over 2,500 births as a midwife. That I have tried unsuccessfully to write this book for the past ten years has been a continuing enigma to me. Why should it be so difficult, so challenging, so heart-wrenching, to write about something into which I have invested so much time, energy, focus, commitment, and passion for so long? Why can I not put into eloquent, flowing phrases the experiences and understandings I have gained throughout the years? To answer these questions is to once again attempt to put into words what I know and what I have learned.

The dawning insight that being a midwife was full of grace and had, in fact, been preparing me to live more fully and more freely was handed to me one warm, sunny spring day by my then out-of-control teenage daughter. (Having survived those times, I can now reflect on them with a little more humor.) She showed me that I had been developing skills to cope with the joys, sorrows, and difficulties of life as they presented themselves to me. And, more importantly, she showed me that there is actually no separation between the spiritual path and the worldly path. She taught me about being present in the moment and about what a tremendous gift that ability is to myself and others.

In the midst of trying to cope as a newly single mother of three—with my only daughter, my youngest, in open rebellion—I found I was not at all prepared for the intensity of the experience. After a particularly violent scene, I walked outside to regain some sense of being an adult. I held a prayer in my heart. I prayed to God to please let me understand what I could do to make this relationship find firmer ground. I wanted to forge a relationship based on love and respect, and I wanted guidance about what I needed to do to bring some healing to our relationship. We were both obviously suffering and obviously isolated in that suffering.

It was in that very moment of heartfelt prayer that time became timeless. A cloudless blue southwestern sky shimmered, and my gaze fell upon tiny purple violets that had bloomed in my flowerbed and, until now, gone unnoticed by me. Space seemed to expand in that moment of utter stillness, and I saw with startling clarity and insight the situation in its wholeness.

My daughter was giving birth to her woman-self, and it was my task to midwife her through the experience with all its inherent struggles and pains and joys. It was as simple as that. I knew without a doubt that I could do this. I had spent years sitting with women who labored for many hours, women who were out of control, women who resisted every part of the process, even women who were uncertain and ambivalent about motherhood, including some who expressed a great deal of anger. This might be a labor that went on for many months or even years, but I knew I could do it out of my love for my daughter and for the woman she would become.

I went back inside feeling very different from the person I had been only moments before. I can only thank God—that Divine aspect that has been present in births throughout the years—for guiding me and revealing the truth once again and for the healing that had begun.

This experience reinforced in a profound way what was, in fact, my purpose in life. I longed to become attuned to right effort and right action, and to be authentic and spontaneous in my expression of love, compassion, and truth from that place of vast sacredness in my soul. I wanted to find the joy in my life instead of identifying so often with the burden. I wanted to live from that wondrous place that had been honed and fine-tuned throughout the many years of being immersed in birth energy. I wanted to come to trust that all of my life was under God's direction and not just some parts of it. In truth, I wanted to surrender to a power and a path greater than myself and my ego.

I yearned for this with all of my heart.

I began to slowly see what I had been given. The truth is that being a midwife has been my way of recognizing that I am a child of God, a divine reflection, and worthy of knowing life's secrets and God's love. It made me aware once again of the magic and mystery of the Divine acting throughout all areas of my life, and it reveals to me daily a place of peace and contentment, wholeness and joy. It is a place that I can return to time and time again for healing, understanding, support, and nourishment.

Therefore, in the spirit of the land where I began to write these words, which holds some of the most holy and sacred places on Earth, it is with supreme gratitude and joy that I offer this in its entirety that it might benefit all beings. Namaste.

Chapter One
The Ground of Being

For me birth is inseparable from all other aspects of my life. It is the common ground we all share as human beings. It is the common ground we share as birthing women. Even as we open our bodies and give new life, we are given the chance to open our souls and give new life. . . new life not only for the one being born but especially for the one giving birth. As a birthing woman you quickly learn the significance of giving completely on every level of yourself so that another life may be given opportunity. Just as woman cannot create new life without the man, the child cannot be born without the woman, woman cannot give birth without the intricate structure of support, support woven throughout the relationships in a woman's life. Key is the connection a woman develops with the birth attendant.

In the birth process, a woman quickly becomes stripped of barriers and defenses. As she bears new life, so does she bare her soul. For me that experience has been rich. The midwife is more than birth attendant. She is friend, healer, mother, teacher, guide to the safe passage of new life, new life in the understanding of who she is, what she can give and the beauty of allowing others to share in a deeply personal and sacred experience.

From the writings of a birth mom

Birth is one of the most magical journeys into the Great Mystery that any woman undertakes in her lifetime. It is filled with endless possibilities. We learn to create a new dream out of a web formed from our own unique experience of living. We are challenged to come into our individual greatness. We question our definition of the truth, that truth by which we live our lives, define our choices, and make our decisions. We become seekers, seekers of a sacred path, as a result of being thrust into the sacred space of the creative feminine aspect of our innermost being. Through this encounter we move into the essence of our being, into a more truthful relatedness with our inner world and outer world alike.

Birth is full of mystery, magic, and power. It touches each of us deeply and poignantly, as an event to be remembered, recounted, and reflected upon throughout our lives. It affects us physically, mentally, emotionally, and spiritually in ways that are both obvious and not so obvious. Seldom are we, as women, more in tune with the natural forces of the universe, both within and without, than during this magnificent and powerful event.

Is it any wonder, then, that childbirth bears such an esteemed and revered place in our lives, even long after our childbearing days have come to an end? It is as if the hand of God reaches out to pour the elixir of the sweetest of nectars, that pure, life-giving substance, upon our tender and parched throats. We open our hearts and souls and reach out to another in the most incredibly blessed and blissful state of love and bonding. Little else in our lives can open our hearts like the innocence and precious sweetness of that tiny little being.

Woman, in her position as co-creator and conduit of this divine energy and life force, is often given in our culture respect, reverence, attention, and acknowledgment by family, friends, and society in general. This experience of the transcendent is never forgotten. It offers an initiation within our being, an opening into the soul, a way home remembered and sought after again and again throughout our lives.

Births are recalled with nostalgic waves of thrill and wonder at best, or with intense emotions at the very least. We remember feeling special. We remember feeling changed. We remember the excitement of being in touch with the unknown. We remember being in awe of a process that was happening both because of us and, yet, in spite of us. We are active participants in this creation, and we are witnesses to a power so much greater than we have known, a power that oversees and guides its completion. We are engaged fully and deeply for perhaps the first time in an adventure called creativity on a soul level.

In my honored position as midwife to this amazing unfolding of experience, I have over the years developed qualities that seemed to have been called forth from deep within my being and nurtured by this birth process. These qualities, such as focus and strength, faith and trust, surrender and integrity, and a spirit of adventure, not only allow us to birth our babies in a state of greater awareness and capability, but also allow us to be parents, partners, friends, and lovers with the same sense of dedication and commitment. They allow us to become midwives to ourselves and our loved ones through all of the daily, weekly, and yearly "births" that we encounter during our journey through this time and space called life.

Our call, in this sense, to be the midwife is a great and ongoing process. While each quality is presented as an entity unto itself, it is, truthfully, only an arbitrary classification, as it is truly impossible to separate one from the other. Each flows in and out of the other like currents in a stream or clouds moving through an endless blue sky. With the idea in mind that similar qualities beckon the midwife and the birthing woman, I shall attempt to weave the threads of these qualities among my own experiences in life, birth, and midwifery. I shall include the stories of other birthing women and other midwives who have been making a similar journey.

BIRTH PROCESS

So, what can say I know about birth with absolute certainty? It happens. It is never the same. It brings tears to my eyes and a smile to my heart. It's a process. It's beautiful. It's poignant. It takes us beyond cultural conditioning and beyond the individual ego. It connects us with women across time and history, past boundaries and customs of country, religion, color, creed, age, and education. It touches us deeply as few other experiences can or do. We are changed as a result of it. I also know that I truly do nothing when I am in alignment with all that is happening. God does it all. I know birth teaches me about myself, as it teaches each birthing woman about herself. And I know that my presence can and does make a difference.

I know that each of the women I have been with in birth has been a teacher to me, offering sometimes-profound lessons and sometimes-simple hints of what is to come. I know that birth carries all possibilities within itself. It is an adventure full of grace and blessing for all involved and is its own teacher. I know that there are no mistakes, no accidents, and that everything happens for the best even if I cannot understand it. I know I can trust the process. I know that life is a miracle within a miracle within a miracle.

It is, in fact, what I do know that has allowed me to make that subtle, yet dramatic, turn from focusing outside myself for the truth to turning within to discover my own secrets of the universe. This knowing has urged me to uncover the mysteries of birth and the magic of relationships as they unfold in my life and in the lives of those I love and walk through this life alongside. Birth has been a most wondrous teaching in "letting go and letting God," and of settling into the quiet comfort and safety of surrender to walk forward through the desert of my past conditioning with strength and courage and commitment.

I am quite honestly amazed at this process that has taken me by the hand through the early years to face fears, uncertainty, and mystery, as well as to meet the joys, triumphs, celebrations, and mystical connections that whisper of all that is holy and divine. Birth is not something that happens to us; it is something that emerges from deep within us and opens us to the mystery. It is about entering into sacred time, slipping through the cracks of the known into the unknown, to meet face to face with the past, the present, and the future. It is about expanding, growing, changing, and becoming. It's about opening our hearts and our minds to more than we ever believed possible. Potential becomes possibility; possibility evolves into a new reality. It is a process that is raw and elemental while also being holy and magical. We are challenged to hold ourselves in our most human form alongside the mystical and God-like soul that witnesses of our essence.

As with any great transition in a woman's life, birth is an initiation. It creates a pathway into the feminine that leads to a threshold, a crossing, a sinking into the depths of darkness that brings an opportunity for more light and more spirit to manifest in our lives and in the lives of those we love. Being witness to this transformation is just as powerful, just as wonderful. It is an opportunity to bring into our lives the power and awareness that all sacred rites and rituals have brought for thousands of years. We can sometimes feel the night wind in our hair, the moonbeams dancing on our skin, the wet grass under naked feet, as they seep up from the past, from ancient rituals, to guide our hearts and souls along a path that women from the beginning of time have entered and walked. It is a path that beckons courage and demands commitment.

It is with this sense of mystery and magic that I welcome you, feeling great excitement and profound joy as we prepare to share the adventure that beckons to the midwife who lives deep within each one of us.

Chapter Two
The Adventure

*D*istant stars in the night sky shimmered and reflected a sliver of moon as I wound around the mountain road late one night, the first day of the new year. My breath caught in my throat as I turned the last corner and saw the lane ahead bordered by flickering luminarias, a traditional southwestern lighting of the holiday season. My eyes followed the curve of the lighted pathway to the top of the hill as I walked up the hill toward the teepee, my arms filled with the bags of birth supplies that I would need. There she was, mom-to-be, laboring hard as she stood under the star-filled sky and breathed in the cold, crisp night air. The minutes ticked away as I kneeled at her side. Her toddler slept soundly inside on the birthing bed while her husband performed last minute chores in preparation for the night to come. Just after midnight, we welcomed this new baby girl into the world, into a dream come true. Her sister woke up just as the baby entered the world. She looked at the baby, held tightly to her baby doll and then looked at me. Precious words spilled forth that touched all of our hearts and souls. Very softly but oh-so-profoundly she whispered, "Thank you for our baby, Karen."

Throughout the years of answering questions about my chosen field, my responses have fallen into similar patterns. Birth is exciting. It's always new, never the same. It's a powerful time in people's lives that I feel privileged to be a part of. Birth is like living on the edge, like driving a racecar, parachuting, or climbing a mountain. Full of mystery and magic, birth touches the great beyond.

I have felt from the first time I watched a baby being born that birth is an adventure; with every woman, every birth, every family, every baby, it is a foray into the unknown. Midwifery feels a lot like being a pioneer on the edge of a vast and incredibly powerful frontier. There is a sense of wide-open spaces where anything can happen. Mystery shimmers forever in the background.

THE CALL FOR ADVENTURE

This sense of adventure has such power to create an experience of myself and of my world. It is the first of the resources that I call upon in birth, in living, in my work environment, and at home with family and friends, or when undertaking the inward personal journey of exploring myself and the meaning of my life. Adventure can take us in its arms and support us as we journey into the unknown. It is in the air we breathe, the food we eat, the sounds of the world that enter our ears, and the touch of our hands as we interact with our environment. It is the "prescription" of our glasses as we look at our world.

As I contemplate the word "adventure," I am aware of and identify with many shades of meaning. Adventure is fun, exciting, and sometimes slightly dangerous. It is encountering the unknown, or meeting uncertainty. It can be seen as scary or as full of tests and challenges. It can be something calling me forth in a new way or something deep within calling to be acknowledged and given a place. It is the juice, the "rasa," that makes life worthwhile and enjoyable.

What is the impulse behind adventure? Although the answer might be different for each of us, my answer is that it is the impulse to move toward something deep within that wants to live life fully, more freely, more genuinely, more in tune with the authentic and spontaneous nature of my being. It is the impulse to uncover more of the truth of my inner state and to give birth to that truth and that state in all of my life.

Jean Houston, in *A Mythic Life*, was forever impacted by Joseph Campbell's *The Hero with a Thousand Faces* at the age of ten. Each story that Campbell told began with the call to adventure, a grand summons beckoning the hero to leave an outmoded condition and journey forth into new ways of being.

Life, birth, midwifery, spiritual journey are all entwined. The sense of adventure can save me by showing the way through uncharted territory, or allow me to flow more smoothly through the familiar with its unique nuances and flavors. At times, however, I want not adventure but safety, security, and only experiences of the already known. I am at these moments out of touch with my sense of adventure, as if I am wrapped inside a cocoon and do not want to be disturbed.

The experience of birth is never the same, and although underneath there is a sense of spacious and flowing groundedness, that is the same in every birth. The unique experience of birth varies according to time, place, individual, and particular circumstances. All of these come together to form the ground of experience, the basis of adventure.

Every woman labors and gives birth according to her own strengths and weaknesses. I used to think that a woman gives birth according to how she lives her life, and, in many cases, I still find this to be true. But I have also come to realize how great an opportunity birth is to achieve potential that might be largely latent, and, so far, untapped. One can give birth to a new aspect of self through giving birth to another. It continually reminds me of the pioneering spirit that led our ancestors from the safety and security of one place into the vast spaces of an unknown land.

BEGINNER'S MIND

An adventuring or pioneering spirit—along with a beginner's mind that is open, full of wonder (wonderful), and flexible as it encounters something unknown—creates a space that potentially draws out the best in ourselves and in those around us. There is a flowering of experience when one is willing to be shown, to be taught, to not know. It has been a powerful and often humbling experience to realize that when I think I know, I am often shown to be wrong; it is when I am willing to not know that the path opens and the way is revealed.

One woman revealed an amazing and adventuring spirit while in labor and giving birth. Noel was mature and quite realistic in her expectations. She read, she asked questions, she took classes, and she sought the advice of many. Still, she did not know exactly what to expect, how her partner would react, or how she would be able to cope. Labor turned out to be challenging, and while not so long in clock hours, it went on far longer than she thought she could bear. Finally, a change of scenery and the addition of another support person that she admired and respected gave her a new perspective and a surge of energy and focus. She walked and walked, back and forth, in the yard by the pool, a grassy enclosed area far away from the city sounds.

The drama of the day was reflected in the shimmering windows that lined the side of the house. When it came time to birth, she gave an immediate response to my question of where she wanted it to take place, inside the bedroom as planned or outside where she had paced back and forth so intently and purposefully. "Outside" was the command. And so, under a nearly cloudless southwestern blue sky, she gave birth to their child directly onto the welcoming earth (via a somewhat loosely defined sterile sheet) as women have done for centuries. It was not planned; it emerged from within the experience itself, coming forth from the depths of her being. It felt like a huge blessing, including the fifteen-second sprinkling of rain from a single tiny cloud passing directly overhead at that very moment. This spontaneous and unpredictable unfolding ignited my sense of joy and adventure, as well as my profound respect for this woman and for the process itself.

PREPARATION

Just as it takes much time and effort to plan an adventure such as a vacation to a remote area in another state, country, or continent, it is crucial to prepare ourselves for the adventure of birth. The greatest teacher is experience; one birth prepares us for the next whether we are giving birth or being the midwife. Even so, pregnancy and birth bring innumerable choices in their wake, more than we are ever really conscious of. These choices are handled best when we pause and give ourselves the time we need for answers to emerge into our awareness. I have learned to carry this pause into all areas of my life, and it is truly a blessing. It gives me time to see a multitude of choices that I have never realized were there, which allows me to make a more conscious decision about the next step. In many cases, my decision seems to appear nearly by itself. As we adventure through our lives and our births, we must make choices about how we view life and the unknown. We must either embrace our experience or resist it; we must either respond to the call for adventure or deny its existence.

CHOICES

There are big choices and smaller ones, but what seems in the moment to be an unimportant choice in the end can change the whole picture. Adventure doesn't mean just letting ourselves be blown about by the winds of chance and change and environment. It calls for us to be aware and awake, meeting every moment as it comes.

One story that touches me deeply held this sense of adventure as well as friendship, trust, intimacy, and focus all in one. The decision to have their second child at home was made after much research, contemplation, reflection, and study. I have discovered over the years that being highly intelligent and well educated does not necessarily go with having a fun, adventuresome, joyful birth experience. Thankfully, there are exceptions to every belief I have ever held.

After a long wait between the time the membranes (bag of water) broke and the time labor began, I found myself summoned from an evening anthropology class and driving at a less than reasonable rate of speed to their mountain home. The labor progressed rapidly beneath a star-filled sky while they were in the hot tub on their porch amidst towering pine trees. In her own words written to her baby about this magical birth experience....

The next hour and a half is a bit of a blur, probably because it sped by in one wave of contraction after another ... each seemingly more intense than the other. ... Karen was speeding down the interstate with her lights flashing, and you, Dad, and I were on the floor in the bedroom trying all the breathing and relaxation techniques we have been practicing for weeks. It didn't take long before I realized I wasn't doing too well in the relaxation department. I was scared and overwhelmed by the strength of the pains and by the speed at which they were coming. "I just can't relax," I panted at one point. "I've got to relax. Let's go down to the hot tub." We decided to make a run for it between the next contractions. ...

Your dad and I managed to hobble down the steps to the tub. I got in and immediately felt relief. "Okay, I can do this now," I said. "This is much better." I relaxed a bit, even joked around with your dad, kissed [your sister] good night. [Grandpa] was inside already pacing. "Where's the midwife?" he kept asking Grandma. Outside we were too busy to worry about it. The contractions were really coming hard and fast.

I looked up a short while later and there was Karen. "Hi, how's it going?" she asked us. We told her about all the happenings at that point. ... I must have let go when I knew Karen was close at hand. I think subconsciously I had been holding back a bit, afraid she would not make it in time, because after she left us on our own, all hell broke loose. One contraction after another hit me. Your dad was great. He kept talking me through them. By this time he was in the tub, too, giving me drinks when I needed them and keeping me well supplied with hard candy to suck on. The woman who thought she'd never make a sound in childbirth started to moan. The sounds came up from somewhere deep inside my soul—somewhere so primitive I couldn't believe they were sounds coming from me. With those deep (and increasingly loud) moans came a freedom, a welcome relief from the pain. I decided at that point that not only was it going to be okay to be noisy, it was going to be necessary. I didn't know at the time that inside [Grandpa] was frantically pacing and growing more and more concerned with each moan that the neighbors were going to call the police to report a murder. . . .

Karen encouraged me through it by telling me to pull the sound up from even lower . . . it really helped. We all joked about disturbing the dogs in the neighborhood. I was pretty surprised that I could still joke and remember thinking I must not be into the "really hard labor" if I could still find things amusing. But the laughter didn't last for long. I guess knowing we had made so much progress in the dilation helped me knock down another psychological barrier. . . .

I don't recall much about the next fifteen minutes or so. I do remember at one point feeling a new sensation very low in my body and wondering what that was all about. I also very distinctly remember a feeling of panic. I didn't think I could take much more and I wondered dimly how much longer it could possibly last. Karen came to the rescue right then. She popped out the back door and cheerily asked us, "Did you want to have the baby out here?" I managed to croak out a no. After a few more contractions she asked me if I felt like pushing. "I don't know what I feel," I moaned. Karen obviously knew better than I what I was feeling because with the very next contraction my body just miraculously took over and started pushing. "I'm pushing, you guys," I yelled in excitement (and fear) ... "Let's get out of here." What a rush of sensations. So much bombarded my mind I'm not sure I can remember all the details. It was sort of like watching myself in a dream. I saw and heard things but I wasn't really there. They floated in my mind and out as I went in and out with each contraction.

They each took an arm and hurried me in the door ... and we climbed the stairs reaching our room as the next pushing sensation hit. I flopped on the bed and let my body take over. In the background I heard Dad saying, "Hang on, I have to put my pants on." I later learned that he was frantically looking around for Karen at that point so he could slip out of his wet suit while she was out of the room. Deciding that the closet might provide the most protection, he dashed inside, practically running over Karen who had quietly slipped in there herself to give him the time to change. We later laughed a lot over that one.

Meanwhile, I'm lying on the bed struggling with the realization that you were almost here. I managed to push away the disbelief, calm down and get a grip on what to do next. Karen and Dad emerged from their close encounter in the closet and started to bolster me with pillows and pads in preparation for what was to come. . . .

We didn't have to wait long. I had barely gotten into position and pushed once or twice when I heard Karen say, "There's the head." I couldn't believe it. We were lucky we headed up the stairs when we did.... While all the confusion [about the camera] was going on, I was pushing with all my might. What a relief it was to actually feel like I was doing something. It didn't hurt that you were a determined little person barreling your way out. Shortly after Karen told me she could see your head, she asked me if I wanted to feel it. I was pretty preoccupied with what my body was commanding from me but I took a moment to reach down. ... Yes, indeed, you were knocking at the door. It made me push a little harder ... with the next contraction I gave a mighty heave and felt you giving way bit by bit. Everyone was shouting encouragement. Karen said, "Here it comes ... ring of fire." With those quick words of warning, I felt the most intense flash of fire, a burst of burning, and your head was out. I remember Karen asking your dad if he wanted to catch you ... he got his chance with the next push. A breath, a bearing down, a loud grunt, and you came splashing out. I felt like my body had collapsed like a balloon. I sobbed as Dad plopped you right up on my chest, your little blue body wriggling and your mouth making weak, then loud cries. ...

Later] as we turned off the light and settled into sleep, Dad and I both marveled at how well it had all gone. We agreed that having you at home was the way to go. It had all been so comfortable, so happy. We had been in control from start to finish. We knew we had made the right decision in spite of pressure from some people around us. You were here, safe, secure, and well loved. You had come out of your warm world right into our own home. What a great way to start your life. We went to sleep knowing that even if we didn't do anything else right in your life, at least we had given you a happy beginning. We found out the next morning that you had given us something wonderful, too, as you began your new life. You slept through the night.

The choice points here are fairly apparent in her telling of the story. As an observer, I can attest to the fact that at every choice point in her pregnancy and birth experience, she and her husband always went for the option with the greater potential, the greater opportunity, or the greater expansion of thought or idea or heart, consistent always with their inner values.

The depth of this relationship and its healing impact on all of our lives has been deeply enriching and rewarding. As important as the sense of adventure was throughout this pregnancy and birth experience and throughout the subsequent birth of their third child, I also speak of it because of the focus that I witnessed in both of these parents. Mom focused inwardly on the birth process while dad focused on her. And even more stunning was the palpable connection between them that seemed to call forth greatness out of the ethers. I witnessed the birth of family, deeper commitment, relationship, personal growth, and healing, and a wonderful opening through which emerged a sense of greater purpose in life to be fulfilled. It was the ultimate in adventuring together, and it paved the way for others to follow if they so choose.

Here is the accounting of the third birth according to Mom:

How the time flies. It's been almost three years since I last wrote in this journal. There hasn't been a week that's gone by since then when I've not looked in my bed table drawer at this book. I've looked at it and thought, "I really need to write (your) birth story before I forget." Well, I never could forget something as momentous as your birth no matter how many years go by. Some of the details may have dimmed but not the memories of the feelings, the sensations, the love. That's all still here and will always be. I still hope to give you the feeling of warmth that came with your arrival.

. . . Each day I would wake up and wonder if today would be the day. There might be some little sign that you were ready to come—more movement, less movement, a little blood, some cramping—everything was heading up to the big moment but it wasn't happening. The week wore on and it got closer to the day [your aunt] was to return home. I had mentally put off your birth so she wouldn't miss it. Now I was ready and you weren't. . . . I started to resort to drinking "magic tea," a recipe my friend had given me for inducing labor. It was an awful concoction of mint tea with milk of magnesia and castor oil. I drank it one night before dinner and ended up with nothing except intestinal cramps and diarrhea. In fact the night before you were born I decided to take one last stab at the tea. I drank a big cup and went to bed feeling nothing except disappointment that there wasn't some action. Only one more day until [your aunt] left. She had to be here for your birth—it had to be tonight!

... By 4 A.M. I was up for good, pacing the bedroom floor, cursing the magic tea. I was never going to drink that stuff again—yuk! It tasted awful and did nothing but give me the runs and make me miserable. Then as I was wallowing in my misery it slowly dawned on me that something in my body had changed. I was no longer feeling pressure to run to the bathroom. Those abdominal pains were different, and low and behold, they seemed to be coming at regular intervals. Funny how labor works. Each time you have it, it is different. There's nothing to compare it to. Having been in labor twice before, I should have recognized the feelings immediately. I was initially clueless. When it finally sunk in—what was going down—I was very excited. You were actually coming after all! All those months of waiting were going to pay off. It wouldn't be long now. [Your aunt[would get to see your birth! All was right with us and the world. All these thoughts went through my head and the feeling of relief that accompanied them, I guess I finally let my body free. I let go and welcomed the process in earnest. I had work to do so By G_d let's get down to it.

I paced awhile longer and waited through a few more contractions to make sure it was the "real thing." There was no denying it now. The contractions were very real and seemed quite intense already. Much more intense than I had remembered with the other two (how quickly we forget)... I couldn't take it anymore. I had to wake your dad.

"I'm having contractions," I said (or something similar). He sat up with a sleepy, stunned look on his face. "Are you sure?" He asked. I told him what had been going on for the last hour. He seemed convinced and excited. He got up and half-heartedly timed a few contractions. I really didn't need the clock to tell me they were coming fairly hard and fast.

Aunt J was groggy but enthusiastic. Ready to help but not sure what to do. She came up to the bedroom to check on me. I told her things were going great. (Karen was on her way.)

Once again I felt great relief and my body let go a little more. I was already having a little trouble and knew it was time to head for the hot tub. It was still dark. Up to this point I was on my hands and knees breathing through the contractions. That always seemed the most comfortable way for me to deal with it. That's the way Karen found me when she arrived. She checked me and said everything looked good. So Dad and I made our way down the stairs and outside. Oh, how wonderful that hot tub felt. It provided immediate relief—that and the fact that Karen was here and I could have some peace of mind.

The sun was just starting to shed light on our intense little scene. It was 6:30 when we got in. In between contractions I remember thinking how pretty it was with the light coming over the horizon warming the top of the trees. I was happy to be having my last baby in the morning. (The other two had been born at night.) I knew you would be a special child to be born with the light of the day. I also remember thinking briefly that I should get up early more often so I could enjoy more early dawn moments. . . .

We weren't in the tub for long (though it seemed long at the time.) I started feeling your little head pushing down. Let me out of here. It's hot, I thought you might be saying. Karen and Dad helped me out of the tub and upstairs. The pressure was immense. I knew you weren't far off now. It was about 7 A.M. . . . By this time the contractions were overwhelming. I found myself singing with each one. It would start involuntarily as a low hum in my throat and rise to a loud note as the contractions peaked. Through the fog I remember thinking simultaneously how pretty/eerie it sounded and marveled that it was coming out of me. Dad was holding my hand cheering me on along with Karen. I didn't think I could take much more. . . .

About 7:30 I started feeling the time was coming to push you out. I told Dad after several more contractions. . . . Then there was one more mighty contraction and I felt like my body was exploding. It was actually the bag bursting and the amniotic fluid gushing out. I felt like I had sent it flying across the room, I pushed so hard. It was about 7:40. Normally, women in labor spend a fair amount of time pushing the baby down the birth canal and out. You were different. I guess you just wanted out. (Your aunt and your sister rushed up the stairs just in time.) Meanwhile, you were heading for daylight. It took about three minutes from the time my water broke until you showed your dark little head. Dad was very excited. He said something like "There it is!" I wanted to be finished. So, when I heard that, I gave one mighty push and there you were. We were all thrilled— me especially! It had been a really intense labor—hard and fast. Looking back on that part, I'm glad. I'd rather have it that way than long and drawn out. I remember thinking to myself, and maybe I even said it out loud. "Thank God I'll never have to do that again!" If you ever have a baby someday, you'll know exactly what I mean.

But beyond the feeling of relief was an overriding wave of joy and awe. There you were, red and slippery. Still attached to the cord inside me. Karen gave you a quick swipe with a towel to dry you off and placed you on my chest. You were so warm and squirming and cute with your dark hair and eyes. Of course, I cried. Of course, everyone in the room cried, too, except maybe your sister who didn't quite know what to make of it all. You even cried a little, I think. Who wouldn't after that scary ride down the tunnel of life? And a fast one at that. By the time you slid onto my panting chest, we knew you were a girl. I was even more happy. My wishes had come true. Our little family was complete. Just the way I wanted it. . . .

What a warm and glorious scene it was. Just as I'd hoped. The sun was creeping in around the shades, you were warm in my arms and everyone around you talked excited about your arrival. You could touch the love in that room! Surprisingly enough, I wasn't very tired. More pumped up by what you and I had just done (with help of course . . .). It's the same kind of feeling you get after running a race or doing some other physical challenge—proud, pleased, adrenaline subsiding, and glad it's over. . . .

I laid in bed upstairs lying face to face with the little bundle of baby yet unnamed. You were so beautiful and peaceful. In spite of the after contractions I was having (that lasted several days!), I had to smile. I wanted to remember you just that way—sleeping warmly by my side. I snapped a picture to remember the moment (as if I could

ever forget) which I still have today. Every time I look at it, those fascinating, powerful, loving hours on the morning of January 15, 1995, come flooding over me. I feel lucky to have had such a perfect birth and such a perfect baby. It's an experience I'll cherish for the rest of my life. All else pales in comparison. Life is a miracle and so are you!
  Love, Mom

FEARLESSNESS

I come to some interesting conclusions if I ask myself what keeps me from expressing my adventurous spirit. My first overwhelming response is fear. Fear of what? Not being safe. Unpredictable means unsafe, at risk, in danger. Fear of making the wrong decision. Fear of the unknown. Fear of consequences, consequences that I would want to avoid at all costs.

I have my attention on how I am doing instead of having an extended perspective. I become self-absorbed, self-conscious. What will other people think? What will I think of myself? It takes me back to my opinions of what life is, what its purpose is, and what it means to live it, express it, and experience it.

I can potentially cross over from a way of being in life that is open and free and willing to be with what is happening in the moment to a way of being that is painfully limited and bound. Life then begins to be heavy, burdensome, a chore, a duty, a debt to be paid to the unrelenting taskmaster. This is the moment when I begin to earnestly pray for humor and humility as it seems to be the only thing that can move me back into balance quickly enough for my liking and my sanity.

This is quite simply a point of fear that I want to move out of immediately, and yet it is a fertile ground that grows lush when explored with patience and humor. Facing this sometimes overwhelming fear eventually puts me in contact with my fearlessness. I am reminded in these moments of a quote I heard many years ago from Ralph Waldo Emerson:

He has not learned the lesson of life who does not every day surmount a fear.

TOLERANCE

There's a tolerance that comes with this sense of adventure as I begin to explore the unknown, and a joyousness that touches my life. When I have truly entered into the spirit of life and what is happening in the moment, there is little that can disturb that state. There is a welcoming of the unknown that transcends usual emotions, thoughts, judgments, and reactions. There is no irritation or annoyance, and no effort to change what is. There is only simple attention to the various nuances of the experience itself, without grasping or avoidance. This sense of expanded and steady awareness allows respect for each person I encounter whether I have an established relationship with him or her or not. I can see in these moments that it becomes crucial to make space for each person in this process in a way that is based on respect and honoring.

When I can move past my fear reaction into this state of adventuring spirit, especially when circumstances might be pulling me in another direction, I begin to lighten up and relax into the unfolding of an occasion of celebration. Things begin to flow more smoothly. I know more effectively what to say, what to do, when to challenge the status quo. Even admitting that I don't know exactly what needs to be done is often enough to move things in a different direction.

INTUITION

If I look at my fear when I am experiencing it, I often want to disown it as if it is a bad or wrong feeling. I jump directly into judging it so that I don't have to feel it directly. If I can look at it more objectively with a more detached perspective, I can often see that my fear is pointing to something I am not paying attention to that may or may not exist within this particular experience. It may be something from my past, or it may be something that another person is experiencing that needs to be addressed in some gentle but straightforward manner. In any case, it is important for me not to make myself wrong for my awareness of the fear. It most often speaks the truth or points in the direction of the truth or is, at least, an opportunity to consciously release an old fear response.

Not long ago I encountered this very fear response quite significantly. It was a quiet Sunday morning following a change-of-shift report regarding a young laboring woman who seemed to finally be making some progress after a long night of minimal change. I walked into the room to introduce myself and to evaluate her progress. In only moments of standing at the side of the bed, I was aware of not just fear but terror coursing through my body. I felt deep trembling inside even while remaining calm on the surface. I scanned the mother, the fetal monitor tracing on the baby and the other people in the room. I could not pinpoint the cause of my concern. The monitor strip was marginally worrisome in light of her minimal progress but not something I would normally respond to in such a vivid and dramatic manner.

I immediately turned the woman over to the physician on call who rather good-naturedly accepted my concerns as valid. A surgical birth followed that revealed a compromised infant that even up to the moment of birth was not reflected by any of the normal parameters we have for evaluating those things. This was, surely, a case of the grace of God as it was transmitted through my body, bypassing my mind and the objective data, to allow for the safe passage of this baby. I felt extremely humbled and full of gratitude to be such an instrument of grace.

In contrast, I had at another time an incredibly fearful response to a longer than normal transitional phase of a mom laboring at home with her second child. I had to go into another room and simply sit with the waves of fear that filled my body until they passed. I kept breathing (who was in labor here?) and accepting the support from my assistants who were both confident that all was fine with mom and baby and that I was going to be fine, too. It was so strong that I wanted to cry or run away or take her to the hospital and never attend another birth. It was, indeed, a very intense reaction, one that is thankfully rare—but in those moments, the feeling of fear could not be denied. While the fear seemed to have no basis in reality and the birth proceeded normally a short time later, I still believe the fear response should never be ignored or ridiculed or judged. If nothing else it may turn out as in this case, where I was able to move some very vivid and painful feelings through my body safely while being surrounded by support.

Sometimes there are births that trigger deep, unresolved issues around our own births. There was a birth that took place a few days prior to my birthday several years ago in which my heart pounded in my chest as I worried about the safety of this baby through a rather rapid first labor and pushing second stage. Another midwife, a close friend, along with mom and dad felt like things were absolutely fine. I didn't. Plain and simple. They wouldn't consider a transport to the hospital regardless of my opinions. I felt trapped, and I was angry. I felt unheard, devalued, and utterly responsible. I wasn't even to the point of suggesting a transfer but they made it absolutely clear that they would not go no matter what I thought. Period.

The baby was healthy and stable at birth and I left their home rather abruptly a short time after the delivery. I was full of conflicting feelings. I knew the parents and family and friends felt I had failed in my ability to see birth as safe and normal. And I knew I had no "defense" technically in light of the normal and healthy baby. I could only honor my own process and contemplate it deeply over time. I could only wonder how much it had to do with my own rapid preterm unattended birth.

At mom's final exam, we talked about it without any real resolution, I felt. I listened to her as she spoke of her "knowing" that everything was fine and that she had truly been surprised at my reactions. I could only pause and speak the truth of my experience. "I wasn't scared for you," I stated. "You were fine. I was scared for your baby." As we looked at each other, I realized that we were coming from the very same place of caring deeply for the well being of her infant. I felt like I was forgiven at least partially, as I was no long viewed as just being controlling or hysterical in my dealings with her. She had a glimpse of my true caring and the sense of responsibility that I felt for her baby.

Fear always deserves respect and consideration while we continually learn how to live in a state of fearlessness and genuine courage. There are few births in which moms do not face their own fears eventually. It may be fear of the pain, fear of being able to go through the labor, fear of letting go and surrendering to that place of not knowing and being out of control, or fear of not being a good enough mother, to mention just a few. It is one of the most challenging points in labor and usually comes near the end of labor, thankfully. It is a time when women need incredible support from those around them to help them walk these last few fearful steps and acknowledge that this is a major life transition.

The moment of birth changes life in a cataclysmic way. We are leaving behind our childhood, our adolescence, and our position as daughter to step into the circle of countless women who have gone before, as well as those who will follow in our footsteps. We are joining the ranks of women turned mothers and we will never see our lives again as we have viewed them before. We will never see our own mothers in exactly the same way, either. Maturity comes knocking at the door and will not be denied entrance. Our mirrors wait patiently for us to see the truth of our transition reflected and to reveal the essence of our humanity. Our bodies, our minds, our hearts, and our souls are molded into something that is quite amazing and often unrecognizable, much to our dismay at times.

THE JOURNEY ITSELF

Adventure can be a call for greatness and expansion beyond our normal sense of identity and limitations, a call for exploration of what it means to live more fully, more authentically, more spontaneously. It may be a call for joy to spring from its eternal source to touch and nurture the true Self. Being my true Self, as Jung and many Eastern saints would define it, would mean being greater than I have, heretofore, believed or known myself to be. A life lived fearlessly is a life lived to its fullest.

Does it mean we will never again feel the surge of fear? Certainly not. But taking that fear and moving beyond it into the next step is the divine adventure. By bringing it to our births as well as our lives in their everyday moments, we will experience even more of life's transcendent potentials. At the very least, we will be giving our children more of their birthright, a right to explore and to be all they can be in this journey through life.

Adventure adds the spice, the juice, the rasa, the energy, the flow to life and living, to relationships, and to our souls. I have witnessed women of all ages and from all walks of life gather to themselves this sense of adventure, to carry themselves and their families through obstacles and heartaches into the unknown as well as into the joy and bliss of everyday existence. It has sustained them through difficulties and uplifted them in the celebrations of life. I know that I am urged from deep within to continue to cultivate this attitude in my own life, and to support it in those I love and am midwife to in all ways.

Chapter Three
Focus

An expectancy shimmered in the labor room as the mom worked long and hard with her contractions. Her husband, her sister, and a niece and nephew surrounded her bed speaking words of encouragement and support while the nurse stood nearby. As the birth drew nearer, I settled onto a low stool at the side of the bed waiting for the time that would call me into moving to welcome this baby. Everyone was doing his or her part perfectly, with the mom directing very clearly what she wanted done, how she wanted it done, and when! As the baby began to emerge into the world, I slipped into gown and gloves and guided this little one into her mother's waiting arms. After the placenta was delivered, I congratulated her and left the room, leaving them to their private celebration. An hour later I returned to check on her and the baby, and you can imagine my surprise as she asked who I was. She spoke the words that reflected the intense amount of focus that had gotten her through the labor. "I honestly didn't know there was anyone else in the room. It was just me and the work I was doing and then it seemed like the baby was suddenly in my arms. I thought the nurse had done it."

The word *focus* will give you a hint about what's coming as well as answer the question of why it has taken me months to even begin to write about it. Single-pointedness. Determination. Concentration. Clarity. Stillness. A cutting through the nonessential. Discipline. Steadiness. Regularity. These are all words that call forth that aspect of mind and soul that may have become lazy or less important since our school days. Athletes have it. Artists have it. Students have it. Scientists intent upon a new discovery have it. Anyone excelling in any endeavor has it. Children learning to walk or talk or tie their shoelaces have it. Yogis, monks, and saints have it. Mystics have it. Animals in the wild have it. Even my very tame and usually timid cat has it when she's stalking a lizard or bird or insect!

For many of us, however, focus may no longer come so easily except in rare moments of absorption in a good book or a good movie, or when timeless, precious, perfect moments touch our lives unexpectedly and we smell a just-bloomed rose, or taste a morsel of something delicious, or feel a soft breeze upon warm flesh. Laziness sets in to sabotage our best of intentions (like all those New Year's resolutions we make). I have bursts of energy and of focus when I can zero in on a project and complete it. At other times I am met by lethargy and I resist the mental effort and discipline it would take to maintain a level of concentration sufficient to completely carry through with a project or idea or plan. I can be my best friend or my own worst enemy in a heartbeat, it seems.

During births, however, I have had quite different experiences. Probably because of the innate intensity of the process, it has been much easier to align myself with the goal and stay present with what is happening in the moment during the course of a labor. Over the years, I began to notice that I was becoming aware of the smallest details and nuances of what was unfolding in the labor and delivery room. This awareness grew larger and I was able to hold an expanded perspective while still keeping the focus on where we were in the process of birthing. A sixth sense developed that knew when labor was too long or too painful, that was aware of the abnormal or the imminent birth. It was through these experiences over time that I came to move from a place of doubt in the early years of training and into a place of confidence and knowing that goes beyond words or ideas, charts or graphs, concepts or opinions.

In some of the most powerful labors I have witnessed, the power has come from the mom's ability to move back and forth with and between contractions with a focus that is single-pointed, determined, and concentrated. The power seems to come from a place of stillness and inner discipline that is balanced with a letting go, a surrender, and an ease with the flow of life as each woman experiences it.

One birth that immediately comes to mind took place in my own bedroom. Beth, in her later thirties, was having her first baby at my home because they lived out of town and she wanted the use of a hot tub for her labor. While she labored throughout the night and into the next morning, I watched her focus with varying degrees of intensity and then completely relax and surrender between contractions. As the birth neared, she focused more deeply and inwardly and then would calmly discuss whether she should go to the hospital for drugs (it was more painful than she had anticipated), focus once again, discuss more options, focus again, and then come to the conclusion that the birth was near, the drugs wouldn't help much, and it was too much effort TO make the trip!! She gave birth with that same focus and concentration and then immediately embraced the baby, a bath, breakfast, the experience in its fullness, and a nap! It was incredibly powerful to watch and participate in it. It was for her a place of maturity and depth, and an expansion of her connection to the essence of life, will, self-effort, and trust in herself.

WITNESS CONSCIOUSNESS

There is a certain witness state, a place of stillness and watching in which I can rest, that lets me shift and sort through all the internal and external data and stimuli. I began crocheting during labor early in my career as a way to still my mind and focus and occupy my hands. Gradually, as I became more comfortable and familiar with that place of stillness and single-pointedness, I realized that in the process my focus and concentration had also deepened.

There is a saying by the Master Li Po: **We sit together, the mountain and me, until only the mountain remains.** I would say that in midwifery "we sit together, birth and me, until only birth remains."

Those times of perfection are still rare, but they never fail to impact me deeply. During these times I am aware that I, Karen, midwife, do nothing. God works though me; God is inside me; God is in the birth itself. I cannot take credit as an individual for what comes as Grace, for the essential truth in those moments. I can only give thanks for the willingness of some part of me to surrender and follow God's will and not my own.

Another poem given to me by a midwife friend is about a midwife who slips away after the birth, leaving the mother to bask in the glow of accomplishment from the work she has done by her own efforts. These words touch my soul so much. That is probably because it has take me so many years to "let go and let God" and not want part of the glory, the credit, the acknowledgment of being someone who makes a difference. Ego has so many disguises.

I seem to have much to learn about serving the Lord. In working alongside the Sisters at the Missionaries of Charity in Kathmandu, those who serve under the direction of Mother Teresa's order, I am struck by their joy, their willingness, their dedication, their devotion, their lack of resistance, and their love and caring for everyone they meet and serve. Their focus is serving the Lord, and their concentration and dedication to their purpose is immense.

On the wall of the orphanage hangs a prayer:

> *Dear Lord, the Great Healer, I kneel before You, since every perfect gift must come from You, I pray, give skill to my hands, clear vision to my mind, kindness and meekness to my heart. Give me singleness of purpose, strength to lift up part of the burden of my suffering fellow me, and a true realization of the privilege that is mine. Take from my heart all guile and worldliness that with the simple faith of a child, I may rely on You. Amen.*

INWARD GUIDANCE

Birth itself may be the greatest teacher of focus, because I have surely seen nearly every woman at some point in her labor shift from an external focus to an internal focus. There are always exceptions—those women who, usually out of intolerable fear, remain focused on the outer world (drugs, support people, medical staff, anyone and anything). Nevertheless, most women reach a point of awareness where we realize that by its very nature, this is a journey we each must take alone. The most loving and caring people in the most perfect environment can surround us, but ultimately, we are the only ones who can do this work. It is often a sobering realization in that it holds true for much of life's work as well as for birth.

Another story that I would like to share took place in the hospital with someone I had no contact with prior to her presenting in labor. In her own words . . . .

> *I have written this note several times in my head, always coming to the conclusion that words simply cannot express the enormity of my gratitude to God that it was you who helped us deliver. I sense that, given the circumstances of*

my condition, had you not been the midwife to help us, I would not have had the birth experience I wanted. ... I truly believe that a higher power led me to [this place]. I would like you to know that this wonderful experience ... has profoundly affected my life. Just as your pending journey came to you in a meditative, spiritual moment, I feel that I was enlightened, or birthed, along with [the baby]. I don't know how yet, or when or where, but I feel something pulling me to become involved with empowering other women [and me] through childbirth. . . ."

Aside from the importance she places on my presence (it was, in fact, one of those experiences for me of "not doing," a place where God was simply present and everything was unfolding in the moment), this couple heard the call from deep within for something greater than they had ever imagined coming forth. Each in his or her own way made the journey deep inside and found through that single-minded, single-pointed determination the strength and connection to the Divine that they wanted and needed in their lives. As you can hear in her words, their experiences of life individually, as a couple, and as a new family have changed profoundly. Birth has the amazing ability to accomplish this. Our relationships with each other have the ability to call this forth.

What we focus on says a lot about us as individuals. It also says a lot about our upbringing, our parents and their values, our culture, our neighbors and friends, our beliefs, our religion or faith, our habits and old patterns, and even our ever-changing images of ourselves and how we would like to be seen by others. Often our unconscious unmet needs and desires cause us to become focused "out there" instead of developing our internal strengths and our true natures. Pregnancy and birth tend to bring a great deal of unresolved issues to the surface for both the client and the caregiver.

BARRIER OF FEAR

To discover for ourselves that we have a choice about what we focus on is as important as being aware of what we are focusing on. In the past year I was shown this in a vivid way by my spiritual teacher. In many of her talks, she has said that many of us are fearful of fear itself while we think we are actually afraid of whatever it is that we are focused on. This in turn stops us from carrying through with right action or making right effort.

In my desire to speak to her personally about a difficult situation I was facing, I was aware only of my fear, fear of uttering words of need and of being vulnerable or appearing foolish, fear of all the possible responses I imagined she might have, of being seen in all my nakedness of being, of being judged and found wanting, of not being worthy of her grace. I was, quite simply, full of fear and my body shook violently as I awaited my time to stand before her. As I came into her presence, I finally trusted both the impulse to speak and the words that I would say enough to accept whatever response and outcome might unfold, trusting that what she would reflect back to me would be exactly what I most needed at that time. And, indeed, what I did receive was a reflection of Divine love and infinite compassion. It is an experience that has stayed with me strongly and vividly not only because of the grace she bestowed upon me, but because I could see so clearly the fear of fear itself and how it feels in my body and plays out in my mind.

Birth has the potential for a great fear to be encountered and released. Birth is intense and powerful. Not so many years ago, there was a potential for mortal danger in birth to both the mother and the baby, and that danger still exists in many parts of the world. Birth inherently contains a force that calls for total surrender and giving up control, a state that many of us fear. It calls for letting go, trusting, and being willing to face the demons of our own making and those given to us by our conditioning. We are challenged to find the forces within us that dispel the negativities and suffering we encounter.

Many of the responses that we hear at the end of a labor may be familiar to you. "I can't do this. It's too much. I can't bear the pain. Please make it stop. I can't go on. There's something wrong. I don't want to do this anymore. Someone please do something. This is too much. This is never going to end." These are words spoken from a place of overwhelming fear, doubt, and exhaustion. And, honestly, they are most often spoken just before the birth becomes imminent.

In the *Course in Miracles*, it is said that everything is either love or fear. Birth brings us to a still point of awareness, a place of choice in which we can either take an irrevocable step of trust into the unknown or cling to the edge of our known, habitual patterns and responses with all our might. We are not only our thoughts, our beliefs, our fears, our decisions. We are so very much more. It is only by taking on this challenge of living from an expanded state that we can determine for ourselves if this is, indeed, correct.

The play of expectations has certainly influenced where and how I have been able to focus. It is still a challenge for me to let go of control, of thinking that I know how things should be or could be, and let the will of God manifest itself. I have come to see that I am not alone in the struggle to come to terms with such fear. It has been my experience that some of the most difficult, long, and exhausting labors have been with women who have issues around control along with fear of letting go and trusting in themselves, their bodies, a higher power, and the process of birth itself. The fact that some women have been sexually violated in either subtle or more obvious ways is another issue that can present itself during birth. If we suppress this knowledge of violation, it can certainly affect the labor process as well as mothering skills after the birth.

Other traumas that can adversely affect labor and birth include being addicted to drugs or alcohol; being in a relationship with someone who is addicted; and growing up in an alcoholic family or a family with violence, including mental and emotional abuse as well as physical assault. It is something I am always watching for if I detect anger, resentment, resistance, or even a state of clinging and helplessness.

Focus for me comes out of a sense of faith and trust in the process itself that I can usually see never lets us down. That does not mean that life goes the way I necessarily want it to go, but once I surrender to the process, I am certain that it will lead me exactly where it is that I need most to go on a soul level.

Another birth that reflects this was a nineteen-year-old having her first baby. I'll call her Jessica.

She was absolutely convinced that she knew what labor would be like ("nothing too bad," "nothing she couldn't handle") and how she could and should take care of herself during the pregnancy. She also had definite opinions about what mothering methods and techniques would be best. It was the perfect "setup" for a long difficult labor, a transfer to the hospital, a baby with colic, and postpartum depression. Well, suffice it to say that she was well into labor when she first realized that these contractions were stronger than the ones she had been having for many weeks. She insisted that we all drive from their apartment to her parent's house for the birth even though she was progressing rapidly. She birthed ninety minutes later in the space she had declared as hers, as she had wanted and planned. She has since had a second child with the same sense of determination, surrender, commitment, will, and focus as she remains true to her own guidance, her own integrity, and her own knowingness.

I was humbled by the entire experience. Why was she the one who brought this lesson of humility home to me? Maybe it was timing, the persistence of youth, our connection in a deeper God-sense of the word, or my willingness on some level to be wrong and to be shown. What I do know is that she lives life with a strong sense of focus, and with an energy that tackles whatever is at hand with determination, forthrightness, and a firm conviction that she is connected to life in a way that will never let her down.

NURTURING

Focusing is a gift that comes from self-effort and is supported by our own particular brand of practices. It may be those named as spiritual such as prayer, contemplation, meditation, and reflection. Or it may be those practices not named as spiritual, like walking in nature, sitting beside the ocean, watching the stars in the night sky, singing a lullaby to a child, holding the hand of a dying friend or family member, or even exercising, yoga, or massage. These all support growth and change and taking the next step into the unknown. Staying mindful of our thoughts, feelings, and environment, and of our relationships with all of life, brings us time and time again to the magic and mystery of living in the moment—for that is truly the only moment we have. The past is over and the future not yet here.

Being mindful of our way through each moment brings joy and possibility, and faith in ourselves and our ability to bear the truth of our lives. It brings energy that we can use in more beneficial ways as we release the contraction that holds and limits our lives to less than desired outcomes. This amazing energy and feeling of "at-one-ness" with our own life, our own destiny, releases so many worries and fears that claim our attention. It truly is the greatest of blessings that self-effort and focus can bring.

Deepak Chopra in *Journey into Healing* provides an insight into becoming more mindful in our everyday lives:

Intention is the active partner of attention; it is the way we convert our automatic processes into conscious ones.

Women giving birth in nontraditional ways take this insight to heart and imbibe it fully in order to face both the unknown and the fears of others. However, any woman giving birth needs focusing, intention, and nurturing in order to move through the process with peace and calm.

Chapter Four
Strength

Karen, after spending that thirty hours of horrendous labor with you, it seemed like a cloud was lifted and [I] was changed in such a BIG way. I think I needed that physical and emotional pounding to realize how lucky and blessed I really am. I'll never forget your quiet and gentle strength....

S trength, courage, perseverance: words that convey that inner substance which we can call upon in times of need to carry us forward past obstacles, pain, attachments, fear, and loneliness, and through the challenges in life that we sometimes would most love to circumvent. Different situations call for different kinds of strength or different kinds of courage, but the answer to the call always comes from a place deep inside that we more or less have access to when we turn our attention inward. As the young woman who wrote the above words experienced, a deep stillness and tremendous strength can be acknowledged and brought forth even when we do not know it is there beforehand. She endured and struggled and wept in the face of the demons she met during this incredible challenge, to finally walk into an amazing light and meet her child and the baby's father in a sweeping love that changed her life from that very moment onward. This is the stuff modern day heroines are made of, women just like you and me.

Strength is the foundation upon which we stand to live our lives with clarity, self-assurance, and determination. Strength is not overpowering, intimidating, forceful, or willful. It is not being overbearing or righteous and attempting to control another, or attempting to have our own way with no thought of the effects on another or the possible harm done to another or ourselves.

Physical strength is a challenge met by nearly every woman who gives birth. And it isn't about having "natural childbirth" without drugs or an epidural or even something restricted to a vaginal birth. We often tell women that this is the hardest work they will ever do. Pregnancy effects changes in every cell in our bodies and in all its systems, from heart rate, breathing, and metabolism to posture, movement, and digestion. It is as if our entire being turns toward nurturing and sustaining this new life. And the process of birthing isn't called "labor" for nothing. We will use muscles we never knew we had. We will probably be pushed past any level of fatigue we have previously known. We will use up our reserves of energy and still be asked to go deeper and find more strength to meet the next challenge, asked to touch the place deep inside that is the reservoir, the fountain of our being.

For some women, it is physical and mental strength and stamina that is called for in birth. One woman who birthed at home had prepared herself for the worst, she thought. Most of the books she'd read and people she had spoken with had indicated that a really long labor was thirty-six hours. So she mentally prepared and told herself that she could do anything for thirty-six hours, no matter how difficult or intense it was. Well, when thirty-six hours came and went, she was thoroughly dismayed to still face many more hours ahead. It took time for her to come to a place of acceptance from the depths of that discouragement and bewilderment. But from acceptance arose patience and the willingness to commit to the work ahead, which did, eventually, culminate in a normal birth and happy celebration. In her own words written shortly after the birth . . .

> *Words just can't express the gratitude [we] feel. . . . The whole experience was so tranquil and natural and we owe so much to your guidance. [We] had an idea of what we wanted for our child's birth but we didn't know how to get there or even if it <u>could</u> be done as simply as we preferred. Thank you, thank you for leading us through everything so gently. [The] birth was so meaningful to us both because we had the privacy and intimacy of our home and each other. We just could not have asked for a more perfect, calmer, more peaceful entry. . . . Our little sweetheart is thriving due, I think, to getting off from such a good*

beginning. . . .

This letter reflects the beauty and joy of the birth rather than the struggles and obstacles that were met and overcome, not because they were not real or valued but because they are contained within a larger perspective of what occurred, the birth of a long-awaited child into their lives. The truth is that most women are somewhat awed by the amount of strength that it takes and by how hard their bodies work to give birth, no less the people who are witnesses to the process. Another woman, who was always very in tune with her body, being a massage therapist, spoke to this issue while in the throes of active labor. Between contractions, she turned to me at one point and exclaimed, *I'm in awe of this body. I have never ever given it enough credit for what it can do, for the amount of power that it contains and how hard it works for me.*

The strength available to us grows over time as we continually and successfully meet the challenges of life, loss, pain, and grief, and as we accomplish the personal goals we set for ourselves, whether earning a college degree, running a marathon, or losing fifteen pounds after the holidays. Living calls for us to go deeper, to strive harder, to have even greater faith in our ability to rise to challenges and to overcome obstacles.

I was in my early twenties when I had my first child, and I was unable to truly integrate all the changes wrought in my psyche and my body during that long labor. It wasn't until eighteen years later that the sense of what my body had been and was capable of accomplishing, indeed, what it continues to accomplish over time, came home to me. I had gone to Peru for a five-day trek along the Inca trail to the ancient city of Machu Picchu, set high in the Andes. The night prior to the trek, I ate tainted food and had to endure a whopping case of food poisoning. I was as sick as I had ever been in my life. Medicines from the trip doctor did little to abate the physical purging until just before dawn. While I wondered how I would ever be able to meet the stresses and strains of such a trip in my current abysmal condition, I didn't even consider not trying. And the next two days showed me my mind and its reactions to life as succinctly and clearly as if God had hand written and delivered the message. There was no way for me not to see my thoughts, my patterns, and my lack of appreciation for this physical body and the opportunities we are given.

My thoughts went around and around while my body took one step at a time. Sometimes that one step was literally all I could take. One step and rest. Another step and rest. A few steps and a longer period of rest. I was so dehydrated that candy wouldn't melt in my mouth in six hours. I wanted to quit. I wanted someone to carry me. I wanted to sit down and never move again. I wished I'd never started. I wanted someone to bring me a horse, or better yet a llama. I wished it would end. I couldn't believe how hard it was, how exhausted I was, how much I hated the pain and struggle. I couldn't believe the amount of support I got from everyone. Suddenly, at some point during all of this, I realized that these thoughts were the thoughts I had had in labor so many years ago (well, not the one about wanting a horse or a llama). And in the end I arrived in camp, long after everyone else to be sure, but there nonetheless, just as I had eventually arrived at giving birth in spite of all my thoughts about the process. My body has a wisdom, I saw, that is beyond me, my thoughts, my mind, and any resistance to life that I might still carry. I was and still am in awe of this process.

The rest of the story goes like this. (I tell it because of the way it impacted my view of myself, of life, and of other women.) A nights' sleep and an offering of celery soup replenished some of my much-needed energy and fluids. The next day was grueling without a doubt, but I managed to stay within sight of the group. I was once again able to watch my mind as I walked and to actually honor my body for its extreme capacity and willingness to fulfill what I asked of it against all odds. It was truly like giving birth again, only this time it was to myself and my awareness of my own strength. It had the feeling of being born "into my body" for the first time. The third day was the most transforming as I was the first one to ascend to the highest pass we had to cross. I had so totally surrendered in my body and my thoughts to this process that I felt the energy from this sacred and holy place reach out to me and literally pull me to the top. Now, whether that was a hallucination from dehydration and extreme exertion and high altitude I'll never know, although truthfully I don't doubt my experience of it. It was a profound teaching that has stayed with me and given me confidence not only in myself and my ability to meet the challenges of my own life, but in other women as well. It feels as if I have been allowed a glimpse of the Divine face of the Mother that resides within each of us, which we can ultimately trust in and turn to in our greatest hour of need.

Here I shall tell you of a woman with the greatest strength and courage I have ever had the blessing to be with in birth. Susan was young, healthy, vibrant, and a delight to be around, fulfilling as she did her dharma as wife and mother to her child with sensitivity, good humor, a down-to-earth attitude, patience, and tremendous love. The planned home birth did, indeed, happen in a milieu of incredible poignancy, intimacy, and love, with an added tangible quality of the impermanence and suffering that is inherent in all of existence in the Buddhist sense of the word. You see, Susan's husband was dying. Knowing this as labor neared, we were each forced to move into sacred ground. I felt absolutely honored to witness the exchange of love between two people who knew they didn't have long to share their lives in this physical world.

This labor was longer than I would have expected of someone having a second child, but I knew that this was sacred time that allowed for an exchange that went far beyond simply giving birth to their child, as treasured as that was in itself. This little one was born into an outer womb of love and commitment born of God, and I have no doubt that it will affect this child all of its life. I can only hope that these words which touch my heart so deeply and bring tears rushing to my eyes so many years later will in some way do justice and honor to this woman and her path as she continues her journey through life. And may it honor these children and this man they call father. Such a person who called forth such depth of love, devotion, and commitment, and who created such a sense of family, can only positively affect our world definition and our experience of what it means to live this life with integrity, courage, and abiding faith.

For me, and I think this may be true for many of us, I have discovered that the more I resist the pain and struggles of life, the less energy I have to cope in the moment. It is a vicious cycle, one that often leads me to despair, despondency, and hopelessness. To bring this back to my analogy of "birthing" while doing serious trekking at high altitude, the next trip I took was nearly as hard on me physically, although without the food poisoning to compound it. I was, however, three years older and dealing with a lot of old emotional wounds when I first trekked in the Nepal Himalayas. And I resisted nearly all of it, although not on a totally conscious level until nearly the end of the trip. The pain. The fatigue. The cold. The effort of climbing straight up with not enough oxygen. The nightmares during restless sleep. I was in tears at one point. (This, I questioned, was my idea of a vacation???) Luckily, I had one successful trip to remember to pull me through. I knew and I trusted that my body could do it. I was, this time, more in a struggle with my mind. And the biggest gift of all came when I repeated the same trek just a few months ago.

Now I was even older and in worse condition physically than four years before. The difference was that I was now strongly seated in my spiritual practices from which came an amazing source of strength and courage. As I sweated and fought my way up those steep slopes at high altitude, sometimes only a few yards at a time, I found that I no longer minded. I actually enjoyed the extreme effort that it took, the feeling of my heart pounding in my chest, the sweat pouring off of me in rivulets, the heaving of my chest as it drew in great gulps of air, the aching of my thighs and calves as they stretched and pulled me up through rocky crevices. What an incredible difference: the resistance dissolved and I felt free and light, with joy rippling through my awareness. I felt the understanding arise within me of how much the painful aspects of my life were simply to be found in the thoughts and reactions of my own mind and not so much in the circumstances themselves. My attitude helps to make my experience whatever it is. My feeling of contentment and joy arises from my acceptance of my life as it is, not as I want it to be as a concept.

This experience has given me much to contemplate. I think that it holds a key for women in birth as well as in our everyday lives; there is a definite mind-body connection that truly affects how we experience the birth process. Resistance is a pushing away of experience, thoughts, feelings, and emotions, or a pulling back from being fully engaged with life, and it takes tremendous energy in itself. It builds a wall between our innate ability to simply let life flow through in all its goodness and badness so that we actually let it in fully. Once that resistance is set into motion, it takes so much effort to change directions. I know that I often miss the gaps which I could step through into another way of seeing or being with what is happening. Much of the resistance in the first place may be a result of our conditioning, our cultural norms, which say we should always be happy; never have pain; never endure suffering, old age, sickness, death, or wrinkles; and never lose our hair or our sex appeal. It may be truly helpful if we each examine what resistance costs us in terms of our own inner peace and contentment, and then study those moments when we notice that we have a choice to change our perceptions. Inner peace and contentment are surely calling me at this point in my life as I move beyond raising children, accumulating wealth or prestige, or reaching the goals of my youth.

The important point it that it is worthwhile to look at some of our most basic beliefs about how we live, how we think life works, what part faith plays, and our usual coping strategies before we actually find ourselves in an intense situation such as birth. It is often too late at this point, when we are floundering and trying to gather to us all our strengths and supports just to make it through. It seems to be a particularly common human trait to vow while in the depths of our pain and struggle to commit ourselves to greater understanding and to developing our good qualities. Then when the crisis has ended, we tend to think that we've made it through by our own will and there will never be another crisis so intense.

Tapping this wellspring of strength and courage actually lays the foundation for other qualities to emerge, ones that draw us out of our immediate concerns with our own lives and situations into concern for others. I sometimes think that it is this very thing which gives rise to the depths of love, caring, and commitment that we experience for our babies as they grow. A woman truly won't see the world the same way after giving birth. Although sleep-deprived, she still wakes at the sounds of her infant. Although starved for some of the activities she used to treasure (long baths, good books, dining out, movies), she thinks first about the needs of her baby and will forego the luxuries more often than not. And if that's not enough, she will often respond to the cries of infants other than her own.

This devotion and dedication lay the foundation for the lives we lead "after the children," the time when we focus on the developing soul within, the emergence of the sacred, the deepest and truest part of ourselves. This love, compassion, and empathy have been historically attributed to feminine, goddesses and mortal women such as the Virgin Mary, Kwan Yin, Tara, Isis, Hecate, Innana, White Buffalo Calf Woman, and the Black Madonna. Love, compassion, and empathy are innate in our being as women and are to be nurtured, strengthened, and called forth as we continue to experience transforming events in our lives. And we ought not forget to be the recipient of them, for we are often so focused on others that we forget ourselves, and then wonder why we feel so depleted and exhausted.

One of the most touching reflections that has aided my own understanding of how strength and gentleness walk hand in hand was shown to me very early in my career by a midwife who had labored at home with her first child for quite some time before transferring to the hospital. Her words follow.

Thank you for everything.... You are a strong and gentle midwife and I am grateful for the strength you gave me in labor.

I have contemplated those words for years, never truly understanding their message for me. In time, I began to notice that I held these two qualities, strength and gentleness, to be mutually exclusive. One excluded the other by their very definitions. I was either one or the other in my evaluation. I began looking around me at women I knew well, wives and mothers, career women, homemakers, other midwives and nurses, physicians and friends. I came finally to see how gentleness and strength are like two sides of the same coin. It is more about bringing them into balance in any particular moment and in any particular circumstance. There are moments when I am too gentle and moments when I am too strong. As well, there are times when someone might tell me I am being too gentle or too strong but then I must look for myself to see if I am being true in the moment or if there is more than what I am able to see in the situation. It is never a static state but always flowing and changing. It is a great learning ground for discovering my own unique way of being in relationship with myself and others.

I have two births that I would like to share with you.

One is a birth I attended at home several years ago. This woman was having her fifth baby at home, never having considered any other option in any of her previous births. This labor was not particularly long, nor was it much more difficult than her others, but at one point she looked at me for a long time and then said that she wanted to go to the hospital for an epidural. "What did I think of that?" she asked. In that moment, I knew that gentle strength was what she needed most, although I didn't think of those exact words. This was something that needed to be explored deeply and with great honor and respect for the process that was taking place.

We talked. She and her husband talked. We all talked together. And all I can say is that there was some magic that happened in the "giving" of the permission to actually make a decision like this without judgment or personal opinion that freed her in a way that affected her long after the birth. It was as if she was allowed to open a secret door and peek in, to step in and "try something on," and once she did, then she could make a free choice to allow the birth to happen in its own way. It was for me a moment of entering the "gap," or pausing, and seeing the value of the choice point in itself. The decision was separated from the choice, allowing a great flowing of energy to fill the space. The birth then proceeded to happen very quickly in the bedroom as she had wanted and planned. Permission to be who we are in the moment, in this phase of our lives, in this particular situation, without masks or personas or ideas, is truly a profound gift to give to ourselves and to give to another by our support, caring, and non-judgment.

Another woman, Kirstie, experienced this in a different way. *Having her first two children at home was a wonderfully rich and rewarding event for her. She got in touch with her inner place of strength and courage and perseverance. Life had brought its share of ups and downs by the time of her third pregnancy. Her health insurance had also changed, making a hospital birth the most cost-effective option. While in labor, she decided to have an epidural, something she had been considering throughout the pregnancy, so it wasn't a surprise. After the epidural was placed, she looked over at me with a look of hope, of fear, of love, and of longing, and she said, "You don't think I'm terrible for doing it this way, do you?"*

My heart was wrung with the love I felt for her and with the recognition of how seldom we are supported and given permission to do whatever needs to be done, with no holding on to our own opinions of how we are or how we look or how we were in the past, with no grasping at some illusive self image. There was no trace of judgment inside me at that moment, nor was there judgment later.– How could there be? I had seen her strength displayed twice before. And she knew it. It changed her life in some indescribable way that balanced the strength and courage with the truth of her whole being just as it opened my heart to the immediacy of accepting what life offers in the moment.

The final birth story that I would like to share speaks of incredible will, strength, and commitment, and an unwavering spirit in the midst of obstacles and the unexpected. Her faith in herself, the process, and her support system; her integrity regarding her own truth; and her ability to focus speak as loudly as any woman I have ever known. In her own words, she tells of her life-enhancing birth experience as it unfolded from beginning to end.

> *Awesome!*
> *I have given birth! I was powerful. I was strong. I was amazing. I was amazed. I have a new force within me. Feelings of strength are flowing through me. My giving birth was incredibly positive and wonderful.*
> *The night that my contractions became regular and I realized I was really in labor, I couldn't get comfortable*

enough to sleep in our bed. The boys were already asleep and [my husband] was at work. I decided to go downstairs and try the couch. I remember thinking about all the women I had read about who chose during early labor to labor alone while their families slept. I felt in touch with those women. With [my husband] at work, my parents next door and the boys just in the next room and none of them knowing what was going on, I sort of felt there was a huge secret only my baby and I knew about. It made me feel special. I was peaceful and accepting of whatever was to come.

My contractions were familiar to me. I had always had back menstrual cramps, and throughout my pregnancy, I had been having Braxton-Hicks contractions. My contractions were a slightly stronger combination of these two familiar sensations. I was not afraid of pain, but I didn't want to anticipate it or expect not to have it. I was trying to let it happen the way it was meant to and not to influence the outcome with my preconceived notions of how my labor should be. I tried to do everything I could to help my body with the incredible job at hand and to listen to what my body needed.

I put a huge bath towel on the couch (in case my water broke), and got a bunch of pillows. The living room was cast in soft light from the dining room. I turned the heater up and the room was warm, glowing, and cozy. Sleep was possible between my contractions when I was supported in a semi-sitting position by my pillows. When my contractions started building, I would awaken. With most of them I could stay in the same position breathing deeply and totally relaxing into them. With others I would have to get up and walk through them while deeply breathing and relaxing. Sometimes I would walk back and forth from the kitchen into the living room between my contractions when I didn't feel sleepy. For extra comfort and uterine stimulus, I made myself some red raspberry leaf tea. I drank that and lots and lots of water all night. I had a huge appetite and kept snacking. I looked at the clock every time a contraction began to see how long it was between them. I don't remember actually ever seeing what time it was. I only looked at the minute hand.

When [my husband] got home from work some time after midnight, I told him I was in prelabor and to get some sleep. I felt that I would need more help later on, and at least one of us should be rested. Also, I wanted to be alone and process what was happening. So, all through the night I had my contractions and learned how to relax into them. That night was comforting and my body taught me how to labor. The next morning I didn't feel tired or drained.

When the boys woke in the morning, I made them breakfast and told them the baby was going to be coming soon. Around nine A.M. I called my midwife. I wanted to be in touch even though I felt it was going to be a very long labor, because my contractions were still fifteen minutes apart and not getting any stronger. The length of labor didn't worry me. I knew I would be able to handle whatever was necessary to give birth. I let [my husband] sleep until I couldn't handle the kids and labor anymore. . . . I took a long, hot, steamy, and luxurious shower in solitude. It was superb to have the water pounding and heating the cramps in my lower back away. I had wondered what I would want to wear during labor. This loose, soft cotton knit dress had come to mind. I decided to try it out; it was perfect, just the way I had imagined. The boys were outside for most of the day. . . . I mostly went inward. At one point, I wanted to go for a walk. We decided to stay and walk around the yard. It was a good idea not to go far because soon I didn't want to be walking anymore. Karen kept in touch a couple of times during the day by phone. We decided she would come and check me after she got off work at eight P.M. During the day, I had taken some homeopathic and herbal remedies for helping labor along.

With my contractions I could feel my uterus pulling down, getting my baby ready for birth. I was most comfortable sitting cross-legged with my back really straight. Pulling air through my nose deeply as the contraction would begin, I would then let my breath fall out of my mouth very slowly and sink into the contraction.

Later in the afternoon, I started to feel my baby's force on my cervix with contractions. It was magnificent to experience my body working the way it was supposed to at such an awesome feat.

All day I felt calm and ready for whatever. I didn't have any ideas about what would happen. I wasn't even excited yet, as I thought it would be such a long time before anything real started to happen. I didn't want to get hung up on waiting for the next thing to happen. I accepted my labor as it came. Mostly, I tried to rest between my contractions. I knew that I would need my rest when labor got harder. Around six P.M. my contractions started to get stronger and closer together. [My husband] asked me once if it was getting worse. I said I didn't want to use negative words like "worse." Then he asked if it was getting more intense; I said yes, it was definitely more intense. My contractions were not painful; they were just requiring more attention to relax through them. As they intensified, I completely quit paying attention to their distance. It was not important. I knew my contractions were making progress, and that was enough for me.

Karen arrived around eight P.M. Right before she arrived, I started losing my mucous plug. Finally, I felt I had begun the long road of dilation. Now I admitted to myself I was in real labor. It was a great sign. I figured I must be at one or two centimeters, maybe three if I was lucky. Karen and I went into the guest bedroom so she could check me. She listened to the baby's heart with the doppler for the first time. During my prenatal care, she had used the fetascope by my choice. I didn't want any unnecessary ultrasound waves going to my baby. We decided to use the doppler during labor. Karen felt more comfortable because we would all hear if the baby was in distress. Using the doppler sort of officiated my labor. We joked about that. I think she checked my blood pressure. Then she checked my dilation. While she was checking, she said, "Oh my god . . . ." I thought, great, I'm not even dilated yet. "You're 5-6 and fully effaced." WOW was all I could think. I had been waiting for it to get difficult. I had thought by this point the contractions were supposed to be getting close to unbearable. I was flabbergasted and nervous. I was apprehensive because I knew she wanted to go to the hospital around 6 centimeters, and I was not mentally prepared to go yet. I figured the baby might be born the next day or probably the day after. Wow. We decided that we would go to the hospital in about an hour. Karen had to call in and see if they were going to be able to do my delivery because my baby was breech. Fortunately, there was a doctor on staff who would do it.

Now I started to get excited. I called my friend, Mary, who was going to go with us. I started to prepare physically and emotionally. I knew that even though there was a doctor who did breeches, we would still have to "qualify" and they would probably still try to pressure me into a second cesarean even though I met all of the criteria for an "attempt" at a vaginal breech delivery. I needed stamina to withstand their "authority." I was strengthened by my caring support people, [my husband], Karen, my mom, and Mary. I knew I could draw from them whenever I needed assistance. During the next hour I focused on my inner knowledge about me giving birth. I KNEW I was going to deliver vaginally to a healthy baby. I KNEW my body was cognitive of what it was doing even if my babies were breech. My main anxiety was the doctor's own beliefs about women in childbirth. I was fearful I would not be looked at as an individual; they would only see me as a statistical risk. I was dreading the possible confrontation with doctors and hospital staff.

It was time to go. I called Mary; she would meet us there. [My husband], my mom, and I followed Karen. Before we left, we discussed how we were going to meet up, where to park, and the possibility of dropping me off at the emergency room entrance. I didn't want to be separated from any of them. I wanted us all to park and go in together. I was scared of being in there without Karen. I didn't want to be isolated with the doctors or nurses at any time. On the way to the hospital, I had a few contractions. We were lucky to get parking near the entrance. We walked right into the main doors. The man at the information booth asked us if we were going to visit someone as if he wasn't going to tell us it wasn't allowed. Karen said, "Oh, we are having a baby," without even breaking stride. We went to Testing and Triage first.

The nurse was cool and distant as she was asking me questions and doing various tests. I don't remember everything that went on because I was centered on my undertaking. I was put on a fetal monitor. They wanted me to lay down during the monitoring, but I wouldn't during a contraction. They agreed to my sitting up. I did have to lay down for the vaginal exam. The doctor really felt around for the presentation of the baby. She wanted to make sure there were no feet under the butt. I knew there weren't. The baby's feet were in its face. I had no room for the baby to have moved around. The doctor said also I was around 5-6 centimeters. They wanted me in a hospital gown; I refused. I was more comfortable in the gown I was wearing and brought for that purpose. We moved into the other room for an ultrasound to confirm the exact position of the baby. I had to lay down for this examination as well. Those contractions were some of the hardest to relax through due to being supine.

The first doctor did a long ultrasound examination, and another doctor came in and did another tedious examination. She said it appeared they would be able to do it. She only had to get a third, the attending physician, to come in and approve.

He came in to do a third wearisome ultrasound examination. I had gotten down before he arrived and was sitting on the foot rest of the exam table when he came in. I was in the middle of a contraction and was unable to say more than "hi." He was eager to ask me questions right then. I sort of waved him away and told him I was contracting. After I got back on the table, he did the sonogram and a vaginal exam to check my pelvis as it had never been "proven" by giving birth. It was painful and humiliating. He said I had a pretty good pelvis. Apparently that is a compliment from an ob-gyn. After his examination he agreed that I was a good "candidate" for an "attempt" at a vaginal birth after a cesarean breech delivery. The second doctor who examined me, talked to me about all of the risks involved in the choices I had, a breech VBAC or a cesarean.

My contractions were holding the majority of my concentration; I was unable to give her much attention. I already knew all of the statistical risks, probably more so than her, and they were what I had based most of my decisions on to try to have my baby vaginally. The rest of my decision was based on what I knew in my heart about what was the right and safest way for my baby to be born. While listening to [the doctor], I felt it was a redundant waste of time.

I gave my birth-plan to the third doctor. He laughed and made jokes about it. I was incredulous of his unabashed rudeness. He did take it and look it over with me. He seemed to think most things were reasonable. . . . We went next to the labor ward. Through Karen and the [female physician], we were able to get a big birthing room instead of a small labor room. Our nurse came in and didn't seem friendly. All of my unorthodox requests didn't help either. [My husband] saved the day by asking her name and telling her we appreciated all she was doing. After that she was much more friendly and helpful. I was "allowed" to be sitting up during the initial 20-30 minutes of monitoring. Thereafter, I had to be monitored for 5 out of every 20 minutes. The nurse was great about letting me stay wherever I was during the monitoring. Either she or I would hold the monitor up to my pansa (belly) to get the heart rate. I was able to take one long awaited and much needed shower. . . .

Different people kept coming in and asking me the same questions over and over. I wanted to lock the door to keep everyone out. This part is really blurry for me. I also looked at the clock on the wall, but I never registered what time it was. I drank lots of water. I also had to pee a lot. [My husband] now had to help me get to the toilet as I started getting more and more tired, but I felt I was on top of everything. I tried to rest as much as possible between my contractions. I was not looking forward; I had no idea of what to expect. I kept working with my body in the here and now. I am unaware of when transition started. My contractions kept getting closer and closer. I started "singing." It was so helpful to make sounds as I was exhaling. It enabled me to keep my breathing slow and steady. I had thought I might hyperventilate easily; fortunately, I didn't have a problem. Once when I was being monitored, my contractions started almost one right after another. This time in between contractions was a godsend. I was able to recharge during the breaks, even if they were only 15-30 seconds. Towards the end of my labor, I had to draw in enough breath to get behind the contraction and push forward with it. I would lean way back while I was gathering enough breath to get behind it, and then lean forward as I sang out my breath. This was hard when my contraction would get started before I was really aware of it.

[The doctor] came in to check my dilation. I was 8 centimeters. The last couple of time I peed I sort of felt like I had to poop. When I told Karen, she came to check me. I was standing up, holding onto the back of a chair. She checked me while I was upright. She said I was nine centimeters as far as she could tell; it was hard to feel the whole cervix because I was standing. It seems the next contraction or the one after I had to push. I had wondered if I would know when it was time to push. A freight train was running through my body pushing. I didn't want to push because [the doctor] had said I probably should not. I roared, "I HAVE TO PUSH!" Karen said, "Okay, do what your body is telling you to do," and she jumped up and came to check me again. She could feel the baby.

The room filled with people. They wanted me to lay down on the bed, so I could be wheeled into the delivery room. There was no way I was going to lay down on the bed. I wanted to walk. I was told women don't walk to the delivery room. I said, "Please, I have to walk." They were reluctantly agreeing and we were half out of the room when another contraction hit. I started pushing; there was absolutely nothing else to do when you have to push. They started yelling at me, "You can't push in the hall! You can't push in the hall!" I moved back into the room for the rest of the contraction. Then we walked down the hall to the delivery room.

When we got there, I was alone with the doctors and nurses. None of my support people were there. I sort of started to panic; it felt like the baby was coming and I was afraid they would not be in time for the birth. Also, I had no idea where they were and why they weren't with me. Karen came first and told me they had to change into scrubs.

The doctors and nurses were telling me to get up on this narrow, high, cold, steel table. I told [the doctor], "You've got to be kidding! I can't get on that bed." I said it over and over again. And they kept saying, "You have to. We are serious." I got up on the bed. I was on my hands and knees. They wanted me laying down which I felt would be unbearable. They finally got me to lay down; then they brought out these huge things that looked like leg troughs, leg stirrups. Once again we began to battle about these. They won. This whole time I kept thinking how absolutely ridiculous all of this was. My contractions kept coming and I kept pushing. [My husband] and my mom came in some time around here.

After I was all flat and stirrupped, my body sort of forgot how to push. I was making a lot of noise during those pushes. Karen helped me to relearn how to push. She told me to hold my breath as I pushed. It was hard but after a couple of contractions, I got the hang of it. All I was aware of was pushing. I heard them say they were going to give me some shots in case forceps had to be used. They kept saying, "Push, your baby is coming." I thought, "NO SHIT, my baby's coming." I heard them say, "We know what it is." I didn't even ask; the sex of my baby wasn't important at all at that moment. My baby's body came out; I then asked what the sex was. He was a boy. [My husband] and my mom already knew, because his testicles came out first.

While they were maneuvering him to try to get his head out, he peed all over me and pooped all over the doctor. They couldn't get his head out so they used the forceps. I didn't even know the forceps were used until some time after he was out. I could feel his head pop out. It was incredible. I felt so powerful. I had only pushed for thirty minutes.

I was exhausted and starving. Finally we were able to go back to the labor room to recover. Our baby started to nurse right away. It was so wonderful to be with him the whole time. He was never taken from us; we didn't let them. I remember glowing and feeling incredibly proud of myself. I kept telling [my husband], "We did it." I felt bigger and fuller; for me birth was amazing.

Not everything went as I had hoped. I am fulfilled by [his] birth. I knew we had to go to the hospital; there would have to be some compromises. The hospital staff was really wonderful for most of my labor. I feel they tried to make things as I wanted. Almost every time I encountered a doctor or a nurse, they told me how great I was doing. It made me feel positive and capable about giving birth. I feel because of the position they made me get in I had to work much harder and the use of forceps was just a way for them to correct their mistake of my position. I have no feelings of inadequacy because forceps were used. I KNOW if left alone, to do what my body told me to do, my baby would have been born without the interventions of shots, an episiotomy, and forceps. Unfortunately, we had to work with the doctors' fears. I had expected that. I, of course, will mourn the aspects that were not as I wanted, but I have no regrets about any part of it. The delivery was such a small part of the superb birth that my baby and I accomplished. I feel empowered. Not only did I give birth to a baby, I gave birth to a breech baby after having a cesarean for my first baby. AWESOME!

Chapter Five
Integrity

I am filled with the fear of this decision, but I know that it is really the answer to my prayers. I have wanted to feel this level of commitment and dedication to my patients; I have wanted to explore the part of myself that holds back and doesn't give everything I am capable of giving. I feel like I'm standing at a precipice and there is no way to go but to jump off into the unknown. What if I'm not good enough? What if I don't know the right thing to do? What if I am too scared? What if I make a mistake? My body trembles and I want to run . . . far, far away from this. It's one thing to be in the safety of the hospital where I've been for so long, and I'm comfortable and surrounded by people and support that I know and trust . . . but quite another to take this huge step into an environment far away from all that. And yet something in my heart yells "YES" and I know that it is the right decision . . . the next step on my journey. God, please help me to be fully present . . . for myself and for the people who put their trust in me . . . and to trust that I will be shown and that I am capable of listening. . . . Do not ever forsake me. . . .

These words were written when I made the decision to begin doing births at home. As much as I was called to do this and as much as my heart wanted to do it, it was still a great challenge that forced me to face many of the issues of my life. Could I be one hundred percent available to others and to myself? Could I carry through as I would need to do to see that births occurred in an environment and under conditions that were safe, giving people the best care that they could expect? Could I be fearless and whole-hearted as I walked this path? Could I really trust the process? I was soon to discover that the answers to these questions lay in truly looking closely at what I thought integrity was, and at how I evaluated myself continually and often harshly to my dismay.

Anni and I had a relationship that long preceded the births of her three children, a relationship that had developed and deepened slowly over the years in an arena of mutual trust and respect. It was this trust and respect that was the basic ground of the relating, the container in which we could explore many of the unresolved issues in our lives. It was because of this mutual exchange of giving and taking over time that we were able to travel to such outer limits of understanding and transformational experiences. Each of her births was an opportunity to explore unknown inner landscapes of relationship, love, connection, and truth, as well as the fear, pain, and stuckness of our human paths.

What I am aware of in thinking about my interactions with her over the years is the sense of absolute trust and integrity with which she lives her life. She has such a deep longing for the truth, and such a profound commitment to the truth, the path, and the journey into wholeness, that everything became the message and the messenger. To look deeply, to honor, to embrace, to confront, and to simply be with the process as it unfolds was her motto. It allowed us both to go deeper than we could have otherwise, I believe. The greatest gift in reflecting upon this is to see that neither she nor I is perfect. There are times when the patterns of a painful past rear their ugly heads and become stumbling blocks to clear communication, intimate and honest exchange, and the discovery of truth and understanding. This gift touches me personally because I identify with having to be perfect in every situation, every encounter, and every role; having to always know the right course of action and the right words to say; and having to have the answers.

There is such a rigidity and a quality of extreme judgmentalism that arises when I contemplate my own integrity, both personally and professionally. I allow myself so little room—let's face it, I allow no room—for error or humanness in living my life and being in relationship. I hate the vulnerability of standing on that razor's edge of not knowing. And it seems that the closer someone is to me, the greater my fear of intimacy, and the more I have to be perfect and make no mistakes. I need to have ALL the answers. Have I given myself credit for being one hundred percent committed to my home birth practice for seven years, twenty-four hours a day, seven days a week? Have I given myself credit for not taking vacations or leaving town without enough prior planning that a client would know before she hired me that I would be gone over a certain period of time? Have I given myself credit for trying always to be honest and truthful in my interactions with myself and others? Have I given myself credit for striving to do my best under whatever circumstances I might find myself in?

Well, the answer is obviously no. I tend to focus on the times when I feel tired or sad or angry that the pager went off to call me away from quiet time or precious sleep. Never mind that I have always been fully aligned by the time I was in the car and driving to the birth! Never mind that I sought to be fully present and available physically, emotionally, mentally, and spiritually during my time with another, even in the light of old patterns being triggered or traumas in my personal life that were touching me deeply. I focus on the times when I am tired and sleepy during a long night's labor, not even allowing here for my humanness and the fact that natural biorhythms are real and affect all of us. I remember the dread of having several women overdue and living every moment on the edge of "not knowing" whether it would work out; I remember planning and worrying how I could responsibly respond to all the scenarios I might imagine in my mind. I focus on the times when as much as I wanted to be fully present and involved, I wasn't due to a variety of internal and external conditions.

So, what do I think integrity is, in truth? Honesty. Realness. Genuineness. Sincerity. Authenticity. Giving to someone to the best of my ability what they have asked of me. The making and keeping of commitments. Being truthful with myself about what I know, about what my limits are physically, mentally, and emotionally. Being strong in holding to the truth of what I feel is the right action or right effort to make. For me it is about admitting my own faults, weaknesses, dark areas, and challenges—if to no one but myself and God. It is being willing to find the courage to work on them even when I would rather not, even when I know that I am walking straight into deep, throbbing pain. I think it involves a great deal of respect both for me and for others. It is an acknowledgment of the vulnerability of not always knowing what is right or best, or what is going to happen next; admitting that someone else may be right or know when I don't. It is about not going into shame or feeling humiliation when I am called on something, not feeling the need to defend myself or protect myself from a painful truth. It is truly about holding life sacred, and holding others sacred while not abandoning myself.

Integrity seems to be an alignment with the truth to the best of our ability to discern that truth in any given moment or situation. It takes a certain degree of fearlessness to give up the strong identification with our self image of what it means to be a good person; a successful person; a valuable person; a spiritual or religious person; a man or woman of intelligence, knowledge, or understanding; a person who is trustworthy.

Being fearless and wholehearted. These are the qualities that have been called forth in my life in a variety of ways that I haven't always recognized at the time. Taking risks that put me on the edge of discomfort, even while knowing I am supported by something greater than my small self, feels fearless. Giving from my heart, even when I know that I will never be met there, feels wholehearted. Courage and integrity. They seem to go hand in hand.

The greatest example of integrity in my life comes not out of my midwifery practice but from my own mother. Several years ago she was diagnosed with breast cancer and underwent a full mastectomy a few days later. There were no complaints of pain, no self-pitying emotional outbursts, no cry to God about the unfairness, no anger or bitterness about what must be. This was remarkable to me in itself. It was as if she had no time to waste by focusing on such trivial pursuits. She gathered her energy to herself and went straight to the core of her incredible ability to align with what life presented her.

The true emergence of this woman's character and capacity to be with the truth and with her own strength as a woman was revealed to me one day in one simple statement during her chemotherapy treatments, which were harrowing in their effects upon her physically. I had told her I was amazed at her attitude of being so aligned with all that had become necessary since the diagnosis, including the surgery, the chemotherapy, the exercises, and the blood tests, as well as the side effects that were so devastating. Her one-sentence response was succinct and profound: "I just decided to <u>want</u> what is happening instead of wanting it to be different."

I was shocked into silence as I contemplated her words. They represented to me some of the highest spiritual teachings I had ever encountered. It was "God's will not my will" that I heard, and it truly surprised me. No resistance. No complaining. Acceptance. Surrender. Faith. (And this from a woman who thinks she does not have a particularly strong connection to God except as an idea.) That statement has become a beacon in my life. No matter what is happening, I try to remember this sense of being aligned with the truth within myself regardless of whether I think of it as good or bad, right or wrong, pleasant or unpleasant. Her integrity in this sense continued throughout this year as she unwaveringly took one step at a time through the experience, emerging in a much more solid and healthy state physically, mentally, and emotionally. She strongly believes in her ability to live life to its fullest, to heal herself. Her passion for living has been ignited and cleansed in the fire of what seemed catastrophic.

The call to integrity was the reason I began doing home births in the first place, as I shared at the beginning of this chapter. During several years of hospital-based practice, I knew that I wasn't being totally available or responsible to others in my relationships with them. This was partly because of the setting and partly because of my inability to give myself fully in commitment. I always held back something—time, money, love, attention, availability—believing that there was not enough for me. I kept my work and my "real" life separate, which created a feeling of either holding back or holding on which certainly affected my ability to go with the flow. And, in all honesty, that seems to be a major factor with many women when laboring and giving birth. A birth that occurred in the hospital around that time truly mirrored my process.

Teresa was having her second baby. Her first baby had been born at term after a normal pregnancy and labor during which she had naturally assumed that everything was fine, as had all of her support people and medical caregivers. The baby was born into her arms and then died almost immediately from an internal deformity which precluded the ability to survive outside the womb. Needless to say, she was devastated. I spent most of her second labor at the bedside, sitting quietly and remaining present with her. While her contractions were strong and close and regular, she still had a prolonged active phase. It was apparent that she was holding back, holding onto the baby and the pregnancy, afraid to confront both the feelings of the last delivery and the possibility of the same thing happening again.

We talked and we waited. We waited some more. I watched the myriad emotions play themselves out until she was finally able to gather enough energy to take the next steps. She needed support every inch of the way and her eyes were filled with terror as she felt the baby emerging into the world. She wanted so badly to hold onto this baby's life. As the baby was placed in her arms, she held her breath while the baby took its first breaths and turned pink and cried lustily. The racking sobs that accompanied this baby's sounds brought all of us in the room to tears.

Now, it doesn't always take something this profound to see that as human beings we often cling to life, afraid to let go and meet our future, the unknown, the uncertain. I have watched women struggle, then meet and come to terms with the situations in their lives in a way that speaks of true integrity, courage, and fearlessness. Observing them has been like being placed inside a peaceful and tranquil garden to witness the blooming of rare and exotic flowers and plants. No matter what the external circumstances were, each woman created a space for the emergence of her unique essence. It is truly a privilege beyond words.

Christina's one of these women whose strength, integrity, and faith has been such a beacon, not only to me but to many people in her life. That she lived over three hours from me did not in the least deter her from her lifelong desire to have her children born at home. Nor do I believe that any external factor could or would have interfered with her determination, as strong and steady as she was. In her unique way of being, I could see that this force somehow merged with a purpose that was, in itself, a curious kind of protection. It always felt like I was entering into a sacred and holy contract with her that fulfilled some sense of destiny for all of us.

And this is not to say that our relationship was all seriousness. We would meet at the Holiday Inn for her prenatal visits, a point equidistant from our homes, and use their bathroom, lobby and parking lot as necessary. I always said it would make a great commercial! This relationship and mutual commitment seemed to call forth greater trust, my trust in her and hers in me as well as faith in God that all would be well. And for me, certainly, it created an arena of highly defined respect and admiration. I shall always be grateful for the path she revealed to me. In her words:

> *I can't tell you how special you have made [my son's] and now [my daughter's] births and pregnancies. You've allowed me to deliver God's way; without pain and suffering, with perfect peace.*

Fearlessness for me, as for Christine, cannot be separated from my faith in God. It's only when I remember that the Supreme Being wants only the best for me, and that I will experience only what He wants me to experience, that I can come to trust this process of life enough to engage more fully. Being responsible and having integrity means having the courage to do what needs to be done in any given circumstance, and then bearing with grace the consequences of all decisions made. Some of these decisions may be popular and some not so popular. It takes great steadiness and equipoise to follow through in light of facing potential praise or potential blame. Either one can pull us off from our own sense of the truth and from right action or right effort.

There is within this realm of integrity the experience that allows for forgiveness. Often we find ourselves striving for perfection and coming up short in our own eyes. Women often feel they need to apologize for "how they acted" while in labor. Measured against this ideal standard we set for ourselves, we can seldom come out a winner, a champion, a warrior. Instead, there is always something we could have done differently or better or with more grace or accomplishment. So much energy is taken up by this internal comparison with the ideal, with another, or with our past performance. It has certainly brought me a great deal of grief in my own life.

When I am being my most critical, my most judgmental, the most unkind to myself, I have to remember to just stop in the moment and "sit still" with all that is happening. In the sitting, I allow myself to focus on my breath, breathing in and out, slowly, purposefully, gently allowing forgiveness of my own "bad mood" to lead me to see a greater truth that I was not seeing. I have to come to regard this state as a call for forgiveness and a beckoning to compassion to accompany me on this journey. Knowing so intimately the ways in which I torture myself in my own mind makes me acutely aware of the need for kindness and gentleness to others. It is a call for true nonviolence and nonaggression, and it begins at home, with ourselves and our own way of being with our inner pain, struggle, tenderness, and heartbrokenness.

From the woman who wrote the beginning paragraph of chapter one come the words that soothe my soul and provide inspiration to a weakened spirit. They remind me that even if I am my most human and make mistakes, lose my faith, or forget to have compassion for myself or someone in my life, I have another aspect that I can draw on to find firmer ground for the moment. This note was written during her pregnancy shortly after moving to another state.

About two weeks ago, I had another bleeding episode. . . . Luckily the bleeding stopped. It really scared me. We went to the hospital and they monitored me for a couple of hours and then sent me home. I had an ultrasound the next day and the doctor feels the edge of the placenta has truly grown over the cervix. So I guess we are probably looking at a c-section. . . .

I miss you so much! I miss your <u>strength</u>! And support. I can't believe how strong you are. I rely so much on that. The medical aspect of this birth scares me. I just keep thinking of you and all that you have overcome, both personally and professionally. I hope I can stand up for myself in the same way.

Thank you for everything you have done for me. I will always be indebted to you for the choices you gave me. Thank you for what you do for women. Without people like you, we wouldn't have a choice. I love you!

There isn't a midwife I know who has not received many such notes, cards, and letters with similar or even more glowing accolades than this. It is truly one of the reasons why we do this work. It is the reward for the soul and the heart, a balm to a weary body or mind. It speaks of the integrity of the profession and allows us to feel our humanness, our connections to each other, and our vulnerability.

One of the most obvious experiences of the need for forgiveness came with a planned home birth of a young healthy woman having her first baby. Marta and I had a close bond right from the beginning, and our visits were full of sharing, laughter, joy, and delight, as well as some deep philosophical discussions about life and relationships. Her labor, however, took me completely by surprise. It was long. It was hard. It lasted all night and into the next day. She worked dreadfully hard and still there was no progress. Her body began to show signs of exhaustion and stress. Through the many long hours, I watched myself go in and out of being truly "present" for her and with her. My focus wavered and I felt utterly unsteady in my faith in the process. The more I tried to focus and remain true to our relationship, the more frustrated and exhausted I became. The more frustrated and exhausted I became, the further away I felt from the essence of the experience and our connection.

When we went to the hospital, I was even more at a loss. Memories of my last transport there of a mom whose baby did not live (see chapter eight) were alive in their strength and potency, filling me with agony and an inner urge to withdraw even more. Still, I knew that there was something else playing at the wispy edges of my awareness, but I couldn't get it. She eventually gave birth by a cesarean to a healthy baby, although the lack of progress seemed to have no cause that anyone could determine.

Several weeks later, I began to have spontaneous memories of sexual abuse as a young child. In talking with Marta later, she admitted to experiencing sexual abuse as a teenager, but that she had thought she had resolved it so hadn't considered it important enough to speak of with me.

I was aghast both that it had not come up over our many hours of discussion and that the synchronicity of my memories of abuse had started to emerge after her labor and birth. Had this labor then been the harbinger of my own abuse memories? Were her "memories" even though "resolved" playing a part in her lack of progress? I don't have the answers or any alas to report, only that they are questions, which call me to explore more deeply my relationships with others and how we are interrelated, and interconnected in ways my mind cannot always fathom.

The forgiveness comes in when I want to condemn myself for not having been able to be fully present as I wanted to be and had promised to be, and for not discovering the issue of her abuse earlier, or when I even take "responsibility" for her having to have a surgical delivery. It is not an easy thing for a perfectionist to give up "control" and forgive herself, necessitating as it does the need to give up blame and shame. It is, however, essential for real growth and development and maturity to unfold.

There have been other instances of not "measuring up" to other people's expectations of me, times when I have been seen as not caring enough, too rough, too insensitive, not available emotionally. Because these instances bring me up against my own need to be right and to be seen as strong and confident, "on top of things," and good and selfless, I am often faced with the task of looking behind the mask of my own making and coming to terms with what is there. It takes a major shift in my awareness to be able to be with someone not liking me or not thinking I am "great," to forgive myself when I don't meet the expectations of someone else, to look deeply for my responsibility in the relationship, and then, finally, to forgive both myself and the other for the "not meeting." Over time, I have come to realize that if I drop down deep enough, I can nearly always see and feel a deep connection and get glimpses of the issues that stood in our way. It is truly a humbling experience, and it can also be exciting in the way it touches the exploration of some of the issues, which keep us separate from each other and cut us off from true communication.

This also is true for many women who give birth. Countless women carry trauma from their births about how well they did or didn't do, or about what others think of them. They judge themselves for making noise, yelling at someone close to them, taking drugs, having epidurals or cesarean deliveries, the baby being breech... the list can be endless at times. It causes such pain that cannot be healed from the outside. I have often been amazed when I talk to women a day or two following their births and they apologize profusely for the noise they made or how they acted. I will in absolute honesty not remember any out-of-the-ordinary sounds or actions or deeds, but I can tell that they don't think I am telling the truth, that I am just being kind. So, I would love it if all women could find acceptance and forgiveness for themselves for any real or imagined breaches of conduct or behavior or lack of perfection. That includes me. It is truly the most healing gift we can give ourselves and each other.

So, in the final analysis, integrity seems to include living life and encountering each moment fearlessly and with a sense of wholeheartedness, embracing all of ourselves and our environment with tenderness and welcoming. It means being kind and gentle with ourselves and our imperfections and creating the space for tolerance and forgiveness for ourselves and for each other. It means opening up the space around all moments and diving into the pause, the gap, to be with what is immediately present as fully as possible. Honor and respect lay the groundwork for this opening, this possibility, while just connecting in our hearts with our humanness for a moment allows the unfolding to happen more naturally and with less effort.

Chapter Six
Surrender

Ripples of light shine forth through people, illuminate other people, resonate with some of them, stimulate them to send forth their own ripples. Some people don't get it just at this time, maybe the light gets stored up or maybe scatters off for other people to find. But the light that shines from a person's heart is never lost, but can only grow and give forth more light through interactions with people, with the natural world, with God. We were fortunate enough to have been shone into by the light of your heart; we are still working on things, very hard, but we are steadfast in our commitment, to each other, to our family, to the light. The same light that you have shared with us to help heal our hearts, is the light that will heal your heart. Thank you.

A note written by a father/husband

One of the biggest lessons to be learned through birth is about surrender, surrender to a body process which we cannot control, surrender to a life change that will deeply and profoundly change us, surrender to a sweeping love that will affect our hearts as little else does. There is surrender of body image, surrender of outer focus, and in many instances surrender of personal desires. There is surrender to labor and surrender to pain, surrender to time and surrender to life's very energy, surrender of modesty and surrender of ideals. So much surrender and so little time!

The above note was written during a period of inner crisis that I experienced prior to making the decision to follow the will of God and not my own. It touched my heart and soul and actually provided the support for the will of God to emerge into my awareness and for the strength of that knowledge to fill my being. I felt like I was surrendering to a force of energy that was not my own and yet that I knew intimately. It flowed over and around and through me, creating a sculpture of a new way of being and of seeing myself in the world. It truly reminded me of how deeply the energy of labor enters into our bodies and souls and continually flows to make its own new patterns and new pathways in the psyche.

"Thy will be done, not my will be done" is the ultimate surrender, the action of "letting go and letting God." How easy it is to speak of, yet often oh-so-difficult for us to put into practice. We want control. We want predictability. We want stability. We want to feel we are in charge of our lives and our decisions. We want to know, to understand, to predict, to be right, to be prepared. We want to be the proverbial Boy Scout, always prepared. I say this, and yet birth teaches another way. It speaks—no yells—of surrender on every level.

Deepak Chopra, in *A Path to Love*, spends a great deal of time talking about surrender:

> **Through surrender the needs of the ego, which can be extremely selfish and unloving, are transformed into the true need of the spirit, which is always the same—the need to grow. As you grow, you exchange shallow, false feelings for deep, true emotions, and thus compassion, trust, devotion, and service become realities. Such a marriage is sacred; it can never falter because it is based on divine essence. Such a marriage is also innocent, because your only motive is to love and serve the other person.**

I cannot predict when labor will commence, how long it will last, when the birth will occur; I cannot foretell surrounding events, the sex of the baby, or how the adjustments to these major life changes will go. I cannot see beforehand what role I will play, what decisions I will be called on to make, or what human dynamics will unfold during the process. In other words, there is no control, no predictability, little stability, little planning, and often no understanding until well after the fact of much of what went on.

Surrender is letting go of thoughts, concepts, and ideas, and even frames of reference to ideas or images we hold of ourselves or another. It involves trust and faith on a level that many of us find uncomfortable for any length of time. I have found that I need to bring myself back again and again with my breath to the moment of now, to trusting that I can, indeed, flow with life and its ever-changing aspects.

The second dream that foretold of a future event, which occurred nearly seven years after the first, was an intense preparation for a birth. The second dream was vague in some aspects, but its essential elements were quite revealing. In the dream, I was accused of crashing into a car in front of a house where I was going to attend a birth. I felt confused and uncertain because I could not remember having done anything that caused such damage to this person's car. I left the scene and made my way into the mom's house. I found myself wandering around the many rooms of the laboring woman's house looking at old photos, artwork, statues, and other personal belongings. I felt quiet and reflective and full of peace; I knew someone was with me but I could not tell who it was. I was called to the front door where there were now police cars with flashing lights and emergency vehicles in front. I kept telling people who came to the door that I hadn't done anything wrong and that I wasn't able to come out because we were soon to have a baby. I felt strong and steady, able to put their dramatic gestures and urges away from my consciousness as I focused on this coming birth.

I was awakened from this dream in the dawn light with a call from the mom, who was actually in labor. The memory of the dream faded by the time I answered the phone. I drove to her house without incident. The labor progressed normally and the baby was born gently and safely into welcoming arms and joyful celebration by mom, dad, and twin siblings. What occurred next was not terribly surprising to either of us because of her past history of cesarean birth with one of the twins. Her placenta was attached to the place of her previous scar and, therefore, with the certain sense that it was not going to deliver in a reasonable amount of time, we agreed that it was necessary to call for emergency transport to the hospital. Expecting to go with her, I was very surprised to hear her ask me to just stay at home with the baby until her husband could return, knowing that she would have to stay at the hospital for a few hours if all went well, and longer if it didn't. She did not want the baby to be taken into that atmosphere; she wanted her to stay where she had been born, her own home where it was quiet and safe and peaceful. I agreed. The dream of the morning returned in all its detail as I walked upstairs with the baby in my arms and watched the emergency vehicles pull away from the house with their lights flashing. I continued to walk around with the baby, showing her old photos, artwork, books, and personal belongings while we waited for dad to return.

I knew that in some subtle and not-so-subtle way I had prepared myself to handle this emergency with extreme calm and foresight, which had actually allowed the emergency personnel to respond in a quiet and honoring manner, more so than I had ever before witnessed. It was truly a lesson in knowing how to create an atmosphere where panic and drama had no hold. I felt blessed to be able to spend these precious moments with the newly born infant and to introduce her to her surroundings in a way that I have never before nor since had the opportunity to do.

These are just a couple of the examples of surrender calling me forward into its gentle embrace. It is not something I find easy to do even at this point, when I have had a lot more practice. I still want to hold on, to grasp, to cling to what I know or think I know. The ability to live in the moment and to flow with the ever-changing is always a challenge. So many times when I think I know what this visit will be about, what this birth will be like, what this couple will face, what path we will walk, I am proven to be wrong; and if I am not proven wrong, then I am shown that so much more can unfold than I had ever imagined might be possible.

Some of the times that I remember most have not necessarily been related to the birth itself. In the guise of midwife, I am occasionally called upon to midwife the relationship into another level of intimacy. As one husband put it, "***Thanks so much for all you have done for us. You have been midwife, friend, supporter, coach, counselor, cheerleader, psychologist, teacher, and mother. You will always be a part of our family.***" This couple (the husband who wrote the beginning note of this chapter) clearly showed me the importance of creating sacred space for whatever kind of "birth" was happening. Just by holding this space, I have witnessed couples making gigantic leaps of faith and commitment in their marriages and partnerships. It is no less of a miracle than that of the birth of a baby. I have witnessed as they have sought to reweave the fabric of their relationships into a garment that was big enough and strong enough to hold a greater vision, a fuller vision, of their lives spent together in family and relationship. These are truly moments blessed by God and filled with Grace.

Many times when I find myself in this situation, I wonder "why." I am not a counselor, nor I am a therapist by training. The only truth that I can come to is that I have cared about their lives apart from their pregnancies. I have cared about the path they walk together. Mostly it has been by grace alone that a sudden shift "happened" and the "container" of their relationship expanded and enlarged and made them aware of even greater possibilities. One couple who came together with this awareness to change the course of their birth experience wrote the following words:

> *You instilled absolute confidence in us that we were doing the right thing and getting the best care; you let us voice our concerns on many different issues and took them seriously; and best of all, you gave us the opportunity to get to know you a little bit for which we'll always be grateful. You're a rare and special person and we truly believe that we were led to you as we began this wonderful journey ... our experience through this was more than we could ever have imagined.*

In the book *Grace Unfolding*, Greg Johanson and Ron Kurtz portray therapists as those who witness a soul, a process, much as midwives do in birth.

> *"Therapists do not create something they can stand back from, look at, and claim as their own. Mindful, nonviolent therapy simply helps us discover and affirm the wisdom of our inner experience. When insights emerge, attachments are released, new roads are discovered, and bodies reshape around more realistic, nourishing beliefs, it is not the therapist's doing. It is not their baby. Therapists' work is more like that of the midwife. They coach nature. When the baby is born, there is no question to whom it belongs.*

Surrender even in small doses has allowed humility to speak to me in some odd ways and at odd times. For quite some time after attending births at home, I began to truly consider that home was the best place for people who were really "together." No sooner had this thought begun to turn into a rather rigid belief that I encountered a woman in the hospital who certainly "had it together."

Sarah was obviously strong, centered, and immersed in love, and she cared deeply about her baby and their coming life as a family. Her husband was incredibly supportive, and I watched in amazement as she journeyed through her labor, all the while transporting each of us beyond our normal beliefs and boundaries. My most vivid memory of this birth was kneeling at the end of the bed as she held onto the squat bar to push with contractions and then her slow graceful movements back onto the edge of the bed. I "saw" her as a Buddha, sitting still and solid upon the earth, giving birth to love and truth. I shall share her own words of this experience from her unique perspective as she wrote these words to her baby a short time after the birth.

> *Sweetheart, you are HERE!! This is the happiest day of my life. No one is more precious to me in the whole world than YOU!! It was an incredible birth, my love. I sat in the bathtub at [the hospital] for seven and a half hours. We went into hard labor at home Sunday morning at A.M. We puttered and finally got to the hospital at A.M. On the way there I said to [my husband] "Hon, just go through those yellow lights." We walked around the hospital till 9 A.M. That's when I decided to get into the tub. Your father talked me through those contractions as we listened to a beautiful Pachabel tape. You'd swear your dad was getting messages from a woman spirit—he was talking me through the pain, as if he knew what it was like to be in a woman's body. He would say, "Welcome the pain. It isn't yours. Let it go." I held on to his every world. He sat on a stool in the bathroom for seven and a half hours. Do you believe it? I was as still as Buddha for most of the time. I felt as if I was sitting in the lap of . . . . me in the lap and you in my uterus. You showed me where you came from—I saw your beautiful soul come into the birth canal. I traveled through the beautiful valley where down below was a dry streambed lined with water-worn rocks. It was an ancient place. That's where your soul came from. I cried to your father as I described to him where you were. I cried as I shared with him the love that I felt for the both of you. He was so*

wonderful. You were rocked in that water for so many hours. Finally at 3 P.M. I got out of the tub and sat on the toilet for about half an hour – that's when [the midwife] checked my cervix (right on the pot!). And we were dilated to a whole 9cm!! One more to go—so we got to the bed (somehow!). The hardest part was pushing. It really hurt. I didn't think that I could do it. I had never felt so powerful in all my life as I did when I held onto that squatting bar and pushed you out like an Indian woman!! Your dad saw you coming—you were crowning for about an hour. One final push and dad caught you as you flew into his arms. I leaned back into the bed and suddenly I had you in my arms (handed over by dad). I cried—a belly cry, and so did you as we lay there for a long time. Dad cut your cord. After about an hour, you and dad went down to the nursery. . . . Your birthday is the happiest day of my life. I'll never forget the feeling of your little body sliding out into the world. My precious [baby] may you be happy all your life.

Some women come through labor with an innate ability to surrender to the birth process that many others are unable to access to such a degree, only to then be faced with a call to surrender to what it means to be a mother. Being a mother in many cases means facing the demons of our own past and how we were mothered; it means looking at mothering in our culture and discerning the "ideals" we profess to believe in and the "realities" of our experiences. It means trying to find our own way through the labyrinth of life—how we would like to be, how we really are, how we might change the world so that we are supported in the ways we believe in, and how we want to be with our children. It is not an easy path, and it's made harder still by many of us no longer having extended families to teach and support and care for us as we become mothers in this world that is changing by the minute.

The following is a story by a midwife who was shocked at the level of surrender and trust it took to walk through the first years of her child's life. Her path was strewn with issues dredged up from the past and from an increased awareness of what it means to be a human being, a loving mother, and a wise woman with a vision of what life and family could be.

It was a path of becoming one with the wounded child within one's own self who is continually in the process of healing and walking on this earth with a deeper sense of one's destiny.

I gave birth at home to a beautiful, healthy eight and one half pound baby boy. My pregnancy went very well—I've never felt better. And even labor was fine. I began light contractions at 10:15 P.M. which got harder, but gently so. At 4:30 in the morning I called my baby's father and he came over. At 7:30 we called my friend and labor coach, and she came over. At 10:30 A.M., I started pushing. And at 1:17 P.M., out came my sweet little guy. It was hard, hard work, especially transition, but it was wonderful, and never was it really painful. It was just INTENSE. He nursed beautifully and we were off to a great start.

But then things turned difficult, and they stayed that way for nearly two years. Looking back, I think I had postpartum depression. I could not sleep. Even now I have had a hard time recounting those early months because they were so traumatic. I was up all night the night I was in labor. I was up all night the night after he was born, because I didn't want him to fall out of bed or go hungry or stop breathing. The next five nights I slept only two hours a night, because he ate frequently and because I was unable to sleep, never knowing if I'd get five minutes' or three hours' rest. Later, even if my son slept for several hours, my engorged breasts would wake me and I'd have to pump, for comfort and for saving the milk I knew I'd need when I returned to work in eight short weeks. Anyway, I've never been a good sleeper—it's the first thing to go when I'd stressed, and go it did.

I entered a dark and scary place. Whenever I'd hear stories about child abuse in the news, I would just lose it. I'd hear the story, and I'd go into it. I'd be in the house the night the boy in [town] wet his bed. I'd hear his fathers' screaming and feel the little boy's terror. The boy was stabbed to death by his father, and I could not climb out of the horror. Stories of starvation in far-off lands, the

Oklahoma City bombing, drive-by shootings, did not affect me in the same way. It was child abuse that destroyed me, and what I felt was not the physical pain, but the terror. A child witnessed a parent murder his brother, and this was more painful that I thought I could endure. The fear, the terror, the wounds that would never, ever go away. I began to think the world was an evil, evil place. I became unable to go anywhere near the neonatal nursery at my job when circumcisions were being done. This to me was abuse.

The only days I felt better were when I'd slept the night before, but I tell you—I rarely slept. My son nursed a lot, I was committed to breast-feeding, and I was unable to ask for help. My son had to be with me. Being separated from him felt like an amputation. Once, my sister recognized my exhaustion and just took the baby from me and ordered me to bed. She went into the living room with the baby. I fell onto the bed crying and sobbing with exhaustion and pain from him being away from me, but I slept. Still, I'm not sure if she did the right thing. I have come to believe the right thing is to tuck an exhausted mother into bed in a small, dark womb-like bedroom, close to a bathroom. Her baby stays with her most of the time, and if s/he is not with her, s/he is just seconds away, with a caring and trusted caretaker who will bring him or her to the mother immediately if asked or if the baby needs to eat. I longed for such a space with all of my heart, but I was unable to ask for this help. Instead, I did too much—I made meals, I shopped, I wrote thank-yous, I made coffee for guests, I developed photos and put them in albums. I never felt manic; I just couldn't relax.

So, what happened? My son gradually slept better. He stopped breast-feeding at 20 months. When he was done eating at night, and I still couldn't sleep, I realized finally that something was wrong, and that now I could do something about it. I went on Prozac when he was 22 months old, and I stayed on it for 9 months. It saved me. Three weeks into it, I could sleep! I tried going off it after 6 months—couldn't sleep. Tried again after 9 months and was successful. As much as it helped me, it robbed me of certain things that I wanted back. Mostly I didn't like feeling neutral about everything. And I missed sexual desire. I also got counseling and discovered two books that were godsends: **Postpartum Survival Guide** *and* **This Isn't What I Expected.** *I devoured them. And even though I didn't have the energy to do even one thing they suggested, I felt less alone. I started asking my postpartum patients about this carefully guarded secret, and could help them with compassion and a good fund of knowledge when they, too, had postpartum difficulties. I began praying and haven't stopped.*

Looking back, I know I've learned something, but what I'm not sure of yet. Should I have had someone else feed him bottles? I really wanted to just do what he needed me to do, but was the price paid too much? I don't know. I do know I need to let people help me, but to this day, there are very few people I trust enough to have around me in times of deep distress. My mother is one of those people and she lives 2500 miles away. I really have only a couple of intimate friends, and in fact, the year I gave birth, I lost my two best friends. This grief is still unresolved. My son's father, to whom I'm now married, I am just beginning to trust. Not that he's not trustworthy, I'm just afraid to be vulnerable. What if I start to ask for help or nurturing and he can't/won't give it? Maybe he is with this strong, does-it-all woman for a reason. Maybe we both need this distance. I doubt it, though. He's very loving with our son.

And the child abuse issues I started working on with a therapist, and some good, solid work has come out of that. The last time I was there, we did some good work and I walked out feeling a weight had been removed from my shoulders, but I know that work is not yet complete. There's more to do, but I feel really clear that this is not the time. Actually, it's just not coming up, and it hasn't for several months.

The progress I've made so far feels good. I've started exercising (after two-plus years), I have enough energy most of the time, I take care of myself (still in solitary ways through reading, and bathing in healing water/herbs/oils), and I've learned to relax enough to take naps often. Sometimes I actually see the world as a beautiful place, especially nature and music, but still not people.

Things are improving. But I am still afraid to have another baby, and still afraid of the work that's coming. Lately, I keep having little accidents. I bump my head while unloading the dishwasher or doing laundry. I scald myself with boiling water. Sometimes my son strikes me or scratches me in anger. And all of these injuries feel like abuse. They make me want to scream. I feel battered and it seems like an overreaction. Sometimes I do scream, which makes me feel awful; I don't want to scare my boy.

I have to heal this part of myself and I know I will. My marriage seems like a safe place to grow, and my son is so wonderful—cute, funny, smart, and very loving. Being with him is the best part of every day. I have a sense of optimism about the future, but I know there's more work ahead.

The intensity of this story plunges me into memory of all those scary places that I can go inside myself and that I have seen other women go both in birth and in psychotherapy. We as women hold such deep histories in the cells of our bodies, our minds, and our souls. Our hearts break and heal, break and heal, over and over again as we connect with the loving and compassionate nature of our souls. We are empathetic as a whole and our path often takes on so much more than what we think we can handle alone. Reaching out to others who walk the path beside us can be a healing in itself as we remind ourselves and each other that we are not alone, we are not abandoned to struggle with huge burdens by ourselves, and we do not face the truth of our lives without the grace of God or Spirit to hold us and guide us. As midwives to each other and to the deepest parts of our own beings, we must come to trust and be gentle with our urges toward greater healing. Trust the process, and be gentle, loving, and kind to all those dark places. And when we recognize our own pain in another, we have an even greater chance to heal with our own hearts those shadowy places inside that we often feel are unique to us alone.

The depth of the healing that has taken place is often not recognized until a later time or until another event in which we see how differently we respond. The midwife who told her story above recently gave birth to a second child, a girl. The birth was intense and powerful, and she felt a place deep within her speak of the universality of this process called birth, and speak of going through this not only for herself and her coming child but for all of womanhood. This little girl brought something with her that allowed her mother to be nurtured, to be healed, and to be more fully present in her experience of this special time. Her story confirms to me that every pregnancy, every birth, and every child is different. Love comes in many shapes, many forms, many levels and bears within it many insights, healings, and blessings. What a magnificent way to have our hearts opened and healed and expanded. Her second birth story follows.

When Karen asked if I'd like to write again, now that I've given birth again, I said yes. And then, I had nothing to write. I'd try and try. But I really couldn't find what I wanted to say. And now I have it!

My second child, this time a nine-pound, 4four-ounce daughter, was born three and one half years after I had my son. The birth story seems irrelevant. Isn't that funny? All I know is that labor was fast, it was really painful this time, and that I was terrified, just terrified, when I was complete. I could not push for an hour, and then I still pushed so gently that she wasn't born for another hour. I was afraid—of the pain I was feeling, of the certain changes to come in my relationship with my son, but mostly of the postpartum. I cried. I screamed her out. I wasn't ready to face what was next.

And it was hard. But I was somewhat prepared, and somewhat lucky. Our family limped through the first thirteen days. I was exhausted, I got very hormonal, rage erupted, and I was at times out of control with my son. But I called for help. The midwives arrived. They rarely left me at home alone. Food arrived daily for two weeks. My house was tidied up, laundry was done. And my mother was due to arrive on day number thirteen. (She would have come sooner, but the baby had arrived a week early.) I started taking St. John's Wort. And best of all, friends took my son for a few hours or the day. He went to the mountains, fishing, and to the mall. My midwife took him for the entire day once, and he came back bathed, dressed in clean pajamas, holding a pot containing seeds he'd planted, and at peace. A gentle heart had cared for him all day and I will forever be grateful.

The lucky part was that the baby slept very, very well beginning at six weeks and my mother moved cross-country to help us!

The baby-my goodness. My love for her makes me laugh out loud. She is something! She smiles constantly and people remark all the time about her happiness. She makes this outrageous deep eye contact with me, my husband, her grandma. The "love look" we call it. You could fall into her eyes. She gazes deeply and with complete and utter trust, yet without intensity. Her eyes love us, and smile at the same time. She is in love, she adores us, she knows we adore her. And it feels so good. It is as if loving so deeply, se defenselessly, is a natural, happy, and even funny thing. And of course it is. It is joy, delight, and bliss. And her laughter makes me want to cry for joy. She bubbles over with laughter.

But, the story continues. Four months old—she stops sleeping well. Hell descends, rage returns, fear triumphs. And, although it took its time, grace arrives. Again, in the form of books. This time they were **I Know This Much Is True, The Unimaginable Life,** *and this unlikely title:* **You Can Be Happy No Matter What.**

I decided to stop thinking about her sleep problem, stop talking about it, stop reading up on the subject, and just ignore my analyses of the problem. Simply stop adding energy to "what is." I also decide to stop taking any of my thinking seriously when I think negative thoughts about my marriage, my husband. I see these thoughts as completely arbitrary now, they always change, and so, who cares about them. I just say, oh hello negativity. Here you are again. Don't let the door hit you on the way out! And then I wait. I don't share my negative thoughts. I add no energy to them. I let the pendulum swing.

And, of course, it's not quite so easy, but it seems to be the right thing to do. Things are happening that make me imagine a life I never before imagined. A life without fear, a life where being in love doesn't fade, a life of peace and contentment all the time! A life spent without defending one's heart. I feel I am still a lifetime or two away from manifesting this true destiny, but I can imagine it now, and I believe I'm on the path.

Regarding my anger, my rage: I know I need my sleep, but when I don't get it, I stop struggling. That alone gives me more energy. I am trying to DECREASE my tolerance for stress, so that I ask for help/take a break sooner.

I have stopped believing what the experts say regarding anything, and especially regarding venting every little thing, examining and thus re-experiencing trauma, and anything that validates NOT loving and forgiving others.

I try (TRY) to live in the present moment. Surprisingly, there is no fatigue, no fear there.

And I forgive myself for my many transgressions from love, and remind myself that I am raising my children in good faith and with all my heart.

And I thank God for my husband, who without any mental or intellectual effort I can see, understands forgiveness, tolerance, and love.

The last story that I would like to share is about surrender and all that it takes to "get there" sometimes. It also points to the theory that life is a spiral and that we continually face the same challenges, the same issues, until we are healed and whole.

Terry was having her third baby, a surprise to say the least, but not an unhappy one. I returned to the States from Nepal just after she had begun prenatal care. I was happy to begin to see her, and I told her that I would be happy to be with her during her birth if I possibly could. I knew that I would be leaving for Nepal about three weeks past her due date, but she had always been on time with her other births, so we didn't worry about it.

As opportunity sometimes knocks in a way that beckons one whether we give our permission or not, I was offered the chance to go work in a neighboring state on the Navajo reservation during the time she was due. My guilt was intense but I felt that this was the right decision for me, financially, personally, and professionally. I hated telling her; a woman nearing the end of her pregnancy is not always able to withstand the shock of change as well as she might under different circumstances. I knew we had the kind of relationship that could withstand this, but it still wasn't easy. We both shed tears that day, but I knew she would be all right and her birth would be wonderful as had her others. She would be in good hands.

So I thought of her often during those twenty-five days and wondered if she had given birth and who had been there and how it had gone. I could never get a feeling of when or how or with whom. I knew, however, that I would find out when I returned home. I was leaving for Nepal on the following Monday when I returned home to work one more day, a Friday. I arrived at work in a rush, tired but happy to see everyone. The midwife who had been on that night expressed surprise at seeing me, and said, "So, Terry is going to be absolutely shocked to see you here." Needless to say, it took some time for me to realize that Terry was being induced that day because of being overdue . . . two and a half weeks overdue!

As that baby was born into my hands, I could only marvel at what was obviously God's gift. Terry had gone through a great deal of emotional trauma and feelings of anger and resentment to finally accept the will of God. She knew that it really would be all right. Never did she figure that it would include my presence at her birth. I would have continued to carry my guilt forever, I imagine. But I couldn't hold onto it in the face of this miracle that truly spoke to my heart that I am not in control of all that I think I am. When we surrender to God's will, then miracles can and do happen, mountains are moved, and the seas do part. I was humbled.

Chapter Seven
Patience

Is there any way I can ever thank you for being there as my support, my sister, my spiritual anchor during the three most powerful experiences of my lifetime, the births of my three children? The truth of it is I can't even fully comprehend the depth of what you have held for me during those experiences. I can't comprehend it but I can feel it running to such deep unconscious places in me and I know that having you in my life and having you present at my births is one of the perfect ways Spirit has blessed me and I am so grateful. Our connection runs strong and I hope to support that as I move out of my birthing phase of life into unfoldment for me and my family.

P atience is about time and about timing. It is about experiencing the pleasurable and the painful, the good and the bad, the enjoyable and the distasteful. Time is not as rigid and controlling as we might think. It can be stretched, stopped, gone in an instant. It can make us feel like we're in a dream when we're awake and like we're awake when we're dreaming. It brings change. It brings us to the edge of an opening to peek at our future. It brings death and it brings life. It shows us the truth and it reveals the illusions of our world. It brings excitement and it brings dread. It brings experience and then a pause and then experience once again.

Patience is that golden nectar of being able to be still in the moment and not want what is not yet revealed. It stops us from pushing the process and forging ahead when we don't yet know which way to go. It allows us to rest in the unknown, in the uncomfortable place of having no goal or no idea of how to get there if we do have one. It takes us out of "doing" and puts us directly into "being." Patience moves us directly into listening, into "the gap" or "the pause." Jack Kornfield in *A Path with Heart* says that this kind of listening opens the doors to a multitude of possibilities:

> *When we listen as if we were in a temple and give attention to one another as if each person were our teacher, honoring his or her words as valuable and sacred, all kinds of great possibilities awaken. Even miracles can happen. ... We must learn to be in touch with something greater than ourselves, whether we call it the Tao, God, the dharma, or the law of nature.*

The births of Hannah, who wrote the note at the beginning of this chapter, were about patience and surrender and grace, and so much more that I, like her, cannot easily put it into words. As our relationship was woven throughout time and experience and opportunity, we were allowed to see and expand into so much more of the landscape of our individual and collective lives. I doubt that I would have seen so clearly the magic, the mystery, and the unique possibilities that exist in each and every moment of our shared time had time itself not conspired to reflect so clearly how Spirit can create and nurture these deep bonds in our lives.

This theme might be reflected in the following words written centuries ago by Lao-Tzu in the Tao-u-Ching as stated in Jon Kabat-Zin's book, *Wherever You Go There You Are*.

> *Do you have the patience to wait*
> *til your mud settles and the water is clear?*
> *Can you remain unmoving*
> *til the right action arises by itself?*

Each of Hannah's pregnancies and births held power, faith, trust, and surrender within them. We shared deeply of our lives and experiences of the time, as well as including each other in our spiritual quests. It was rich and rewarding. Her first labor was hard but filled with magic as she labored and gave birth underwater in their hot tub. She was surrounded by loving, caring people who walked through this experience with her in a way that was respectful of life, of the process, of Spirit, and of her particular unique journey. Tears flowed into the water as we all celebrated this birth and the making of a family. She felt the triumph of power that flowed through her veins as she met each contraction and pushed her baby out into the world. She felt the energy of total love and support as her marriage was made even stronger through this shared commitment to their path.

Here are the words she wrote after this birth:

> *An appropriate beginning for a new journal. I had a little boy yesterday. To describe it as incredible and awesome is such an understatement. Reality feels and is completely transformed. My life is not the same. My heart feels so full for this little one and I fear being inadequate, not able to meet the huge responsibility of this little life placed in my hands. I feel traumatized by labor and yet as each moment passes the intensity of it fades into this kind of holy mystical grief. It feels like in some way it was a very ancient initiation. So mixed in with the terror and the pain is this tranced-out visit to a very sacred place. Can it be true that just one day later I'm feeling the gift of this journey when yesterday I was feeling betrayed, afraid, and would have done just about anything to have avoided it. Strange stuff. It seems there is something to having to bring our children in with such intensity. Is it a spiritual initiation into motherhood creating a bond between mother and child that doesn't ever weaken. It is definitely powerful and beyond any experience I will probably even have again except perhaps my own birth and death. And to this little one, may our days together be very blessed. May our loving connection blossom and grow as I get to watch you evolve more and more into yourself.*

Her second birth was faster and even more powerful as she once again labored and gave birth in the hot tub surrounded by faithful friends and family. In many ways, I think that her ability to simply be with the issues that arose one by one throughout her pregnancy gave her the ability to be with the pains and frustrations and challenges of motherhood. Both postpartum periods were difficult, as she had babies who did not relish sleeping in any predictable manner. She sought healing of her body and soul as she struggled with the sleep deprivation and eventually triumphed once again.

Once again she shares with us her second birth as written in her journal.

Here I am by the creek again waiting, waiting for this baby. I hope it will be soon (like tomorrow). My mother comes in tonight. I'm excited to see her. It's been perfect today getting some time alone. Feels very rejuvenating. . . . Love is the song that resonates in our soul = that just came to me sitting here. Did the meditation last night and feeling that vibration throughout and around me was very special.

Oh, dear baby, I hope I get to meet you soon. I feel like I really can't wait any longer even though I know if that's your choice I'll just have to. I just really want to hold you and dress you in those little clothes. I want to share with my mother the joy that you bring. It feels like hanging out with you and your brother is a real gift to me. There will be the times of fatigue and frustration but let me always remember the preciousness of your life, the gift of being given you and your loving. . . . the fun, the joy, the total awesomeness of watching a little one grow and grow. May I do right by you, guide you as you need. Center in my loving and the joy you bring, the playfulness. This world has its harshness, the rough edges. Let us live together in the knowing that there is God here, there is heaven on earth and there is peace within. It is my quest to stay centered, to keep a God focus, to be aware when I step off the path and to get right back on again. Already you've taught me these lessons. Help me to be open to your needs and creating the space you need in your birth and throughout your life. I am so thankful and feel so blessed to be preparing to receive you. You very special one most precious. Come to me soon."

I regret not finding the time to write in here sooner. The baby is almost 3 weeks old. WOW! I feel I'm beginning to adjust. I'm keeping up with the treadmill at least. Her birth was so perfect, so beautiful. Labor started between 3:30 and 4 P.M. while grocery shopping with my mom. When we got home I timed the contractions for about an hour. When they had been three minutes apart for one half hour I called [my friend], [my husband], and we called Karen. My mom decided to stay with us during the labor. Which I wasn't sure about at first and now I am so grateful for that.

... feels [like] that's why everything turned out as it did (her coming early, me thinking the baby was coming early, etc,). I feel it healed a lot for both of us. So I dusted while [everyone] had dinner and then we walked around the park. It was a beautiful evening out and there was a glorious sunset. We walked for about 45 minutes. I guess labor got more intense during that time.

I returned home just as the intense stuff kicked in—this must have been about 7:45 or 8 P.M. I went into the bathroom. . . . and labored alone for 15-20 minutes. . . . and then slowly made my way to the hot tub. On the second set of steps in the greenhouse my water broke and I threw up. I then made it the rest of the way to the hot tub and it felt like heaven! Such a relief. I then journeyed deep into labor land. I found that if I kept focused on Spirit it kept me on clouds floating just above the pain. It required continuous vigilance to do this. I called in Christ to be with me and was reminded of the crucifixion. I chanted different names. Not sure what they meant but it felt like they were different names of God. . . . it was very special, so much Spirit. Karen came at some point. And a bit later Betty came. I could feel it the minute Betty pulled into the driveway—her presence was so powerful and reassuring. Then the pain got more intense (which didn't seem possible). It got hard to stay connected and not get pulled into the pain.

Then I felt myself pushing and it hurt a lot. I just prayed please make it quick. I think I pushed two to four times in the water. Then suddenly I wanted to get out and stood up and leaned against the greenhouse wall and pushed two more times (at the time I thought this must be the fetal ejection reflex Michel Odent talked about and then reminded myself to stay out of the neocortex). The pain was incredible, a lot of burning as she moved so quickly out and then her little head was born and I pushed again and her shoulder came out and there she was. They handed her to me through my legs and I sat down and floated her in the water. My little girl. I was so high and she just lay there blessed out with one hand on me the other floating in the water. Right away I wanted my mother and [my friend] ran to get her. It felt like I was a child, perhaps a new baby, myself calling out for my mother and it was so nice to have her there. We floated in the tub thirty to forty minutes til I stood up and delivered the placenta and the cord was cut. I then took her and held her in bed. [My husband] and I had some alone time with her and then everyone came in and sang her happy birthday and we had chocolate cheesecake and wine. Before that she started crying a lot and we couldn't figure it out till I started to nurse her and then she was happy.

She is such a sweet baby. She seems quiet in a strong and spunky way. Her eyes are very clear and friendly. I really love this little one. What a special gift she is and what a gift her birth was to me. It was everything I wanted, easy, peaceful, spirit-filled. Sunset outside, the greenhouse filled with candlelight and full of people holding God's light. My mother praying in the living room. Such a beautiful, powerful experience for me. Writing about it fills my heart with loving, with gratitude to God for the blessing of my dear baby. Gratitude for my family. . . . it's a quiet breezy peaceful evening. . . . such a treat to have this time alone.
. . .

It was the third pregnancy that told the tale of our connection and how Spirit can work so mysteriously even without our expressed consent. She became pregnant while I was living in Nepal. I kept having strong images of her and I remember once wondering if they were, indeed, going to have another baby. As Spirit would have it, I suddenly had to return to the States many months before I had planned, due to circumstances beyond my control. I returned to find that she was expecting a baby in about eight weeks. I was surprised and delighted and readily agreed to attend her birth. We both shed tears at this unexpected gift of sharing another birth.

She faced many issues during the time I was gone, one of them being "mother stuff" in which she was very angry and disappointed in me for being gone. These kind of feelings can be experienced strongly even when one can intellectually understand that it is all-perfect. (Another woman felt this same sort of feelings even more strongly before I left, having known for many months prior to her getting pregnant that I was leaving. It didn't stop the anger or frustration that surfaced even while she totally supported my journey.) Hannah grieved but trusted the process enough to know that things were happening for a reason. So, here we were pulled together by a timing that neither of us could have planned had we tried.

The indefinable and unexplainable occurred during the course of her intense and wild labor. It was an early spring night when she called, a night full of raging and howling winds, rain, thunder and hail, snow and sleet. She labored in the hot tub on the porch while a fire burned in the wood stove inside. She rocked and moaned with the wind and we talked about what this baby was bringing with it—the raw elements with all their power. There really isn't any adequate way to describe the intensity of this labor or the challenges it brought. She progressed rapidly but the baby remained high and in a posterior position. She felt lost and unable to "know" what to do, such a contrast with her other experiences. In fact, it was so unlike her other births that she couldn't believe it was really happening. In the midst of all this, the rain poured, thunder and lightening rent open the sky, the wind ripped through the valley, and the fire crackled and burned in the den, sending dancing fingers of warmth and light into our awed minds and hearts.

I had to trust that things were going to be fine even though I, too, had my doubts. The other midwife who was with us was great support, a rock, a haven, as she had had several labors herself just like this one. Patience seemed to be all there was along with a heavy dose of trusting in the process. It is my usual way to "follow" women throughout their journey providing safe space and encouragement; this time, however, I felt like I was being called to follow her into a place of darkness and "voidness," catch hold of her hand, and then to lead her back out into the light. I had the distinct image of Moses leading his followers out of the desert. I felt great amounts of fear in my body. What if I couldn't do it? What if I was wrong? What if I couldn't find my own way out? I could feel the vast potential _and_ the deep level of love and caring and connection that existed between all of us present. I prayed with all of my heart for God to be with each of us taking this journey. It felt like we were lost in the "gap" or the "pause" I talked about earlier with no clear sign of how to emerge from it into the light of day.

I began to move into directing, giving her very clear signals about what to try to effect some change. Nothing seemed to work and I questioned my resolve. There were enough abnormal signs to make it very challenging for me to hold onto my beliefs. Finally, she got back in the hot tub and continued to push. I once again held the space. It was a true test *of patience. I somehow knew that it was about time and timing and yet I couldn't define either of those in these torturous hours. Then her strength filled her, and with great resolve of her own, she said, "That's enough. . . . . I want to go to the hospital." I agreed but urged her to let me check her to see if the baby had descended any further even though she didn't feel that it had. With great joy and not a little surprise, I told her that the baby was ready to be born with just a few pushes. She was shocked; I was thrilled. And, indeed, the baby was born a few minutes later. WOW! was all any of us could say. The storm outside abated for awhile only to dump several inches of snow later on that late spring day.*

Her words written after this birth reflect once again the intensity of the process and of what we all experienced that night.

> *Thirty-seven years old today. . . . I find/make time to come up to the creek with my little baby. Life is packed—it is so busy and so intense. . . . [The kids] are acting out a lot. . . . definitely the babysitting I got for them today was the best gift in the world. The gift I gave myself.*
>
> *[The baby] is a real sweetheart; cuddling him and being with him is such a gift. I'm not ready to have him be with a babysitter yet. He sleeps all night cuddling next to me. It took me three children to just relax and let myself bond this completely with my child. It feels very good, very right.*
>
> *His birth was so intense. I guess I should try to write about it but I'm not sure what to say. At 7:30, or was it 7, labor started as a storm started to build in all directions around us. Dilation went quickly and I was able to ride to intensity, feeling the support of God and of those around me, my beloved midwife, Karen, my friend and husband, and Kathy, the midwife assistant. At 10 P.M. I was ready to push and that's when everything went wrong. . . . I lost my internal sense of what to do. I lost my inner connection with Spirit. My body was reverberating with such severe pain. There was no way to know what to do with it. It was like being trapped inside a terrible storm with no way to escape. I kept asking to go to the hospital. A cesarean seemed like the only way out and yet I didn't want that. I just wanted out of my torturous body. As I went through*

this the storm outside met from all directions and swirled above me with winds, hail, sleet, lightening, and thunder. Our hot tub was outside, so there I was in the middle of two storms, one externally and one internally (the external one was strong enough to blow the roof off a school nearby). I was totally lost. I had no idea what to do. Everyone was giving me all these suggestions, do this, do that, do this position. None of it worked. They kept trying to turn him and that didn't work. Meanwhile the incredible pain kept coming and coming. I finally went back to the hot tub and pushed with everything I had. During this time I kept chanting "Get thee behind me Satan." I felt I needed spiritual protection but I wasn't able to feel that my prayers were answered. I asked [my friend] to call my spiritual healer friend and my teacher for spiritual healing to ask for their prayers.

Then after half an hour or an hour in the tub, Kathy told me I should get out. I said and I felt very clear, "I've given this all I can and I can't take any more. If I get out it's to go to the hospital." Okay everyone said. Karen just needed to check me. So I went inside and she checked and felt a head. What a miracle. I had given up believing this baby was going to be born. I gave a couple more pushes and there he was, a little baby boy. I was too exhausted to look at him but they lay him on me and my heart chakra just exploded. It was so nice to have him there on the <u>outside</u>. What a blessing. And [the kids] got to come see their new brother and we all got to cuddle. Then I was so glad we were at home and so grateful to have my little baby boy.

Patience during this labor and birth process was a subtle form of "doing" for me. It was filled with moment-by-moment reflections as I was never able to completely relax and let go into believing things were just going to be one way, either okay or not okay. I was forced by circumstance to face each second, one at a time, and evaluate how things were simply in that moment. And then in the next moment once again evaluate. Living in the moment suddenly became filled with new meaning, although I felt like "patience" was something forever beyond my grasp.

Pushing the process is something spoken of quite frequently in counseling. I define it as "making *it* happen" before *it*'s ready, like trying to make bread rise faster by lifting the towel to look every ten minutes instead of just letting it be, or like trying to make the cake cook faster by opening the oven door every few minutes. Instead, we find that we lose the momentum or heat that has been building or happening naturally as it is supposed to, in its own timing, thereby losing some or all of the ground we have been gaining.

Patience in birth is seldom something that comes "naturally." Moms want it to be over faster because it hurts or because of fatigue or because their last labor went faster or simply because they thought it would be over long ago. Families want it to be over faster because *they* thought is would be over long ago and because it can be very difficult to watch someone we love and care about endure pain. Fathers often describe a "helpless" feeling that is nearly intolerable in some cases. As partner, lover, husband, mate, we join the other, the Beloved, as a companion on a journey that often seems to take us to the underworld of shadows, fears, and dark nights of the soul. We are challenged to find our own meanings and depths as we watch and participate in the unfolding experience. We are each tested over and over, moment by moment, to know who we are and to feel how deeply we can care.

My first experience of this came when I was a labor and delivery nurse. My closest friend, Janie, gave birth five months after my first child was born. I was back at work on the unit where she, too, planned to have her baby. I went in with her and her husband on my day off, acting both as her nurse and as another support person. Her labor went through the night well into the next day with very slow but steady progress. I was as exhausted as she was. So was her husband. At one point I examined her and she had not made much progress over many hours, although there was nothing really wrong at all. I left the labor room abruptly and stood in the middle of the nurses' station surrounded by my fellow workers and burst into tears. Her husband came out and found me in this state. Obviously thinking something was wrong, he was beside himself. I could only shake my head and say that no, everything was fine; I was just exhausted and didn't want it to be taking so long. I had never been so close to someone during labor and wasn't prepared for how much I wanted to help her and how helpless I felt.

From that moment on, I had real empathy with families and friends as they became tired and frustrated, even angry with those of us who were supposed to be "doing something" to help this laboring woman. It truly is a challenging position and one that many of us find uncomfortable.

I was attending Suzanne who was having her first baby. I knew her as a friend long before she became a client. It was delightful to share the journey of pregnancy with her and I was happy to be able to be with her and her mate during her labor. It, too, was long and extremely painful, more painful than it should have been, I knew. The baby, I realized over time, was stuck in a posterior position (face up instead of face down) making for a long, hard labor. Each of the things we tried from multiple position changes to drugs to the epidural to augmentation changed nothing. When the decision was made for a surgical delivery, her husband became irate. The anger was explosive and pointed at each of us involved, and yet it didn't really feel personal at all. Because of my relationship with them, I think, I had a moment when time was suspended and I could see the place of fear and pain and true concern for what his wife was facing that turned into a rather stunning attack on those providing her care. I have never since reacted to the anger and frustration I have witnessed in family members in quite the same defensive way as before. I can now see their concern and the fact that we are really coming from the same place, the place of wanting things to go well and for mom and baby to be safe.

There is an aspect of patience that supports calmness. Many of the letters and cards that midwives receive or that are sent to the birthing center contain phrases such as "you were so calm and that allowed me to relax and trust that everything was going to be all right;" "your support meant everything;" "you were all so kind and caring;" "I will never forget all of you for making this special event in our lives even more special." These are directed at the nurse, the midwife, the physician, and any of the other support staff. They can be from women who experienced normal labors and births, from women who experienced something unplanned like a cesarean birth, or even from moms who experienced a loss.

I remember one dad reflecting upon what he had witnessed and experienced when his wife was taken for an emergency cesarean because the baby's heart rate plummeted without recovery, making an immediate delivery necessary. He confessed that he had been terrified inside for the safety and well-being of both his wife and their baby. When he had looked at each of us who were quickly making decisions and moving accordingly, he felt such reassurance because of the purposeful yet calm movements that we were making. There was a definite sense of urgency but such focus that he knew things were going to be all right. And they were.

These words of his made me pause and actually recreate the experience. I could see how all of us had not only conserved our words and actions to what was absolutely relevant and important to the situation, but that we had also explained and included the mother and father in what was happening. It took the edge off the sense of uncertainty that they experienced. There seemed to be a quality of patience in those movements and explanations that slowed time and allowed us to all adjust to the sudden change in experience.

Patience comes from dropping down deeper and deeper into any moment and being able to wait in the stillness for the next move to unfold, even giving up the idea that there is a next moment to wait for. For me it seems to come out of the ground of trust, trusting the process, trusting something I call God, trusting that I will be shown exactly what to do and when to do it. It means not trying to figure it all out or make things happen. It means "letting go and letting God," that place of surrender that we talked of earlier.

It seems that patience is also letting go of expectations, those ideas of how life or people should be. It's knowing less and embracing the mystery more. It is "allowing" for life to be just the way it is instead of how we want or need it to be. Many of my most humbling experiences have come with labors that seemed to be going "nowhere," labors without progress or descent of the head, or labors that were "stuck" at a particular point for many, many hours no matter what we tried to change them. I am frequently amazed at how often I have "thrown in the towel," so to speak, and then had the birth happen rather uneventfully a short time later. In the beginning years, I was embarrassed when this happened and ashamed of myself for giving up so easily (even when it was many hours that had passed). In time, however, it has simply become an opportunity to find humility.

Some of the families whose stories I have shared with you have taught me much about patience in ways that were totally unrelated to their births. It is not something that can easily be put into words as it is more of a felt-sense when I have been in their midst. It comes across in the way they talk to their children, the way they show them or guide them or even discipline them. It comes across in the way they feed them or hold them or comfort them. Patience seems to have such a quality of honor and respect for life itself.

One of my favorite patients was blind and had been for many years. Watching her move about in her world was an amazing experience for me. I watched my own inclinations to try to make things easier for her, to pick up things. But as I spent more time with her, I finally started to relax and to let her set the pace of our visits. I found myself in less of a hurry not only in her presence but also at home by myself. I suddenly found myself savoring the taste of food, delighting in the smell of a newly blossomed rose, actually feeling the tingling in my fingers as I folded the silk and cotton and velvet of fabrics of my clothes, drapes, linens, and household items. I felt the coldness of ice and the heat of hot coffee as I swallowed. I would not at the time have thought that she was teaching me patience, but that is truly what I feel now. It was a way of slowing down and experiencing life as never before.

Most people do not experience these same kinds of awareness during labor, although it does happen and it feels like a gift always. I was called to a home one early evening with someone having her first labor. It was a cold, wintry day followed by an early night. Still, it was warm and cozy inside their home. Macho, their old sheep dog, followed Sheila from area to area as she walked through every contraction. She would pause at the end of each wave and take a deep breath, inhaling not just oxygen but her whole, entire experience, us in her outer world and all the sensations of her inner world. These are her words.

It was the most beautiful and rich time in my life. I felt like such a real woman, larger than life. . . . like the Goddess herself. The contractions were never painful, just intense. It was like a deep squeezing that took me to the core of my being. I could feel myself reaching deep down to meet my baby and opening the door for his release into my

life. I looked out and saw [my husband] and felt his support, and how much I loved him washed over me. I could almost feel how the three of us, me and the baby and [my husband], were all together in this moment of time waiting for the time when we would begin our lives in a new way. And I saw you and [your apprentice] sitting there, coaching me, encouraging me, believing in me, and I was so filled with the beauty of it all. I loved to watch the candles ripple in the slight breeze of the room. ... Everything seemed to shimmer and glow and bless the beauty and power of this night. I could imagine women throughout time who had walked and walked and waited and waited for their babies to be born. I felt so lucky and so happy to have had this experience. I definitely want to do it again.

This labor wasn't long in clock hours, but I could see how moment-by-moment we were brought into more expansive ways of being together. She would stop at the fireplace and reach out and touch the cool stone of a bear fetish and then move on and stroke the cording on the edge of the couch. She paid attention to everything that caught her eye or her touch as she walked so gently through this labor. Even during the last stage, which was more difficult that she had thought it would be, there was still gentleness and a savoring of "BIRTH" as she now knew it from the inside. I wanted to follow behind her and touch the same things she touched, gaze at the same things she gazed at. It was truly like I was being given a seat before an open window in which a new soul was arriving and I could watch the journey as closely as another human being ever can. We share this night in remembrance each year of the baby's birth. It has one of those magical feelings about it as if the fairies came or the angels descended to touch our cheeks, like a picture book of childhood which comes alive with the telling. She dreamed into the magic, and gave us who were there with her a glimpse of that magic.

Patience is expressed as freedom and strength in some of the ancient spiritual scriptures. It is linked to discipline and comes from deep faith and awareness in God, and it is a quality that matures within one's own being. When we practice patience, we are also practicing respect; we are allowing it to develop at its own rate and in its own timing. In the scriptures, we are urged to develop the kind of patience which allows us to pause, to breathe, and to find the comfort and ease of our being before we perform our actions, actions which support the glory of God.

I have another story that is a classic illustration of how patience comes with practice over time and comes out of committing oneself to the development of tolerance. Belinda is a mother of five now, and I have been with her for the past three pregnancies and births. When I met her, she had two children under three and was expecting her third in a few months. She had just moved to town with her husband, her children, three cats, two dogs, and a goldfish. They found enough acreage to allow everyone enough space to roam. That was good. It was summer. That was bad, in the hot, dry smoldering heat of the desert. They had moved from the northwest, making the contrast even starker. I began to dread our visits, but not because I didn't like her; in fact, I liked her a lot and felt very close to all of the family (well, maybe not the goldfish. . . .). I felt like I had known them for a long time. The fact was that she was tired, bone-tired, she was pregnant, she was hot, and she had the kids alone from early morning until her husband came home late in the evening. She had no friends or family available as she had previously, and neighbors might as well have been across the world instead of across a field. She unpacked and cried, unpacked and cried. She missed her family and her support system of many years. Her patience was stretched to the limit. The simplest request from one of the children seemed to drag her beyond her ability to cope. She tugged at my heart, but it was difficult to witness her frustration and lack of patience with life, with the little ones, and with her husband, who was working very hard to get them settled and to cope with his own challenges—of a new job that offered great potential.

I alternately worried about and resisted my relationship with her. I didn't want to be the babysitter; I didn't want to be the best friend; I didn't want to be her mother. I was her midwife, but the edges seemed to blur and shift from visit to visit. I felt trapped and I began to lose patience.

Her birth had a dream-like quality. I arrived near midnight to find her moaning loudly in the bathtub, candlelight flickering in the window and the lights of the Christmas tree in the next room reflecting in the mirror behind her. It was another night of magic. Within a short time, she pushed this beautiful newborn out into the world via the water and we all cried together. It was Christmas Eve. We all kneeled down in silence around the bathtub, gazing at and holding this precious baby in our love-filled eyes. It was a hushed silence and the wind against the windowpane seemed to speak volumes. It changed everything and to this day I cannot tell you why or how, only that it happened. Grace by the want of any other name came to rest and ease the aching hearts of this family, me included.

After several months, Belinda tried to put into words what she had experienced that night.

> *I felt the gentle emergence of my baby, and in that moment of awareness of where I was empty and full at the same time, I knew that I had a choice to make. We were being given a very special gift through this baby and I must either accept it or deny it. I chose to accept it. I felt a gentle wave of relief wash over me, almost a physical wave, nearly orgasmic, that made me feel like I was coming home to myself. I remember looking up and seeing the love in the eyes of [my husband] and my children who were sleepy-eyed but excited and seeing how beautiful and loving you were sitting there against the wall looking at all of us. It's like I saw with new eyes that life is very, very precious and sweet and oh-so-short. I wanted to be there every single moment of my life for this baby and for my other children, too, and to give my husband the love and support for being such a good man and father. I saw how I had been holding back, resenting, and afraid to embrace this new life, wanting for things to be as they had been, for us to be in a different place, for me to have what I had left behind, thinking that was better than I could ever have here. I felt like I had been living in a barren land and then I opened my eyes to see how full and lush my life and this land was actually. I suddenly felt the magic of opportunity and possibilities that I hadn't known existed. I wanted to be here, right here in the middle of the desert, and to make a new life, a full life, one where we can each be full and happy being a family.*

Their lives did not change on the surface, but they certainly changed in ways that made it a joy to be with them. It's not so much that she lost all of her impatience or stopped having moments of frustration and anger; it was more that she was able to be with those feelings as they arose and still maintain her connection with the kids, the animals, the new baby, her husband. I had my own unique place in their lives, one that I could open my heart to and embrace. We could sit on the porch with iced tea in our glasses and look out over the mountains and enjoy the companionship and the silences. Patience seemed to be palpable in the air itself.

Patience is something I believe I will be striving for my whole life; it doesn't come naturally or easily for me in my everyday life. I reach ahead into the next moment, or I find myself clinging to this moment for all it's worth. However, I have precious glimpses of patience when I am "going with the flow" during a birth, and I remember them when I am impatient in traffic, in a line at the grocery store, or because I'm on hold for more than a few minutes. I can only continue to practice patience and wait for the time when it becomes as natural as breathing. I may have a long time to wait, but then again, what a noble goal is patience.

Chapter Eight
Life As a Blessing: Acceptance

I just wanted to tell you how much I enjoyed your support and friendship throughout my pregnancy and birth. You are a wonderfully warm, funny, loving person and I feel blessed to have met you and shared this incredible experience with you! Your calm, confident attitude and beautiful smile helped make this birth the best it could possibly be. I like to tell the story about how you came in and started reassuring me it was okay to push before you even checked me! You knew what was happening as soon as you walked into the door! You're so good!

When I experience birth (giving or supporting) I'm reminded of God's love and power. Babies are truly perfection and holiness personified, and I praise Him for the three He's entrusted to me. Thank you for being a part of our little piece of Heaven!

Words of a new mom

Have you ever been around people who seem to exude faith and confidence in life no matter what circumstances prevail in their lives? They seem to have the ability to accept the unfolding of events, situations, and happenstance on such a deep level that it appears as if they exist above and beyond all that is happening, while still managing to live life fully with enthusiasm. It is an "in the world but not of the world" quality that expresses the Divine in both subtle and not-so-subtle ways. Nothing can shake their faith or trust, and they thereby accept as a blessing all that life has to offer. Their awareness is truly that everything happens for the best and everything is due to God's will.

These people are always a blessing in the lives of the people around them, even if the reasons are not recognized or understood. They offer gifts to the rest of us simply by their very state of being. The saintliness and earthiness that dwell within their hearts combine to create humor while merging the qualities of purity and worldliness. This special elixir of sweetness and richness embraces and enfolds all who come into contact with them. In my experiences, I have had the great fortune of meeting with quite a number of these people. They have allowed me to see and embrace the blessings in my own life and to come forward and be present in all my own greatness. The key ingredient for me, however, has been the awareness that they have also included my faults, my bad moods, my bad habits, and my shortcomings, while loving and honoring and valuing me as a unique human being and seeing me as a child of God. They have welcomed me, accepted me, loved me as they have welcomed and accepted and loved all of life as it has presented itself.

One of the most personally touching and profoundly vivid experiences of this that I can offer comes from a birth where I was attending to a couple for the third time, their soon-to-be eighth child. Now, there aren't a lot of couples that I could honestly encourage and support to have an eighth child with all my heart and soul, but Kathy and Dan were such a couple (see chapter 10).

Because of Kathy's complete faith in God, life, and the birthing process itself, and because of our shared experiences in attending other births together where Kathy served as a lay midwife, we were able to focus on aspects of her pregnancy, birth, and family growth and change that I seldom have the opportunity or time to explore. Our visits in her home took us on "adventures" that could have never been planned or orchestrated by anyone except the Divine. There were forays into the unknown and uncharted territory of the complexities and meaning of modern life, marriage, family, commitment, and the eternal search for truth, God, and Self. Dan's presence at the visits altered the content at times, adding joy and lightness on a level that speaks of the deepest honor and respect, which continues to touch my heart in a way that inspires and nourishes my whole being.

It was really no surprise, then, that this birth brought such incredible blessings. It was here in the early morning hours that I witnessed the pure and powerful welcoming, respect, and nurturance that a couple devoted to

God and the daily imbibing of these values can provide to each other, to their children, and to anyone else present. This was by far the longest and the most difficult of the three births I had attended with them, but it was not worrisome in any sense. The lesson came as dawn began to lighten the night sky and the other children began to awaken.

One must imagine the physical setting in which this birth takes place. It is their home, a small three-bedroom house where rooms are shared and space is a precious commodity. The miracle revealed itself as each child came into the room where mom was actively laboring. Each of them, from the eldest teenage daughter to the youngest toddler son, was greeted with such individual respect and acknowledgement in a way that honored his or her unique place in the family as a special and important member. Each was recognized as a part of this birth, for the part he or she would play, while including any feelings about the birth and this coming child that each might be experiencing.

Space suddenly shifted in a real and dramatic way and I saw and felt that they lived not in a small house but in a spacious mansion, a palace that included more than enough room for each child to grow and develop into the fullest God-being possible, according to each one's talents, strengths, and inclinations. I was moved to tears o watch what felt like a sacred ritual of an incredibly intimate and loving exchange.

Shortly thereafter, their little baby girl arrived to truly welcoming arms as each and every member of the family, me included, took turns holding her and speaking words of gratitude and joy at her arrival. Their true state of honoring and respecting each other reached out and lifted me up into a place of Grace, and I, too, was welcomed and witnessed as a special and integral part of the family. In a way that I cannot describe or explain, I felt a miraculous healing of the trauma I still carried surrounding my own premature birth so many, many years ago. It was as gentle and complete a healing as I ever could have imagined.

And as I gathered my belongings to leave their side, I knew that this is the most blessed of gifts that we can give to ourselves, to our children, and to each other as human beings, this tremendous sense of humor and respect and allowance of great inner space. It is the ground from which our greatness can spring forth, the place from which we can be nurtured and fed and sheltered until we are ready to walk forth into the fullness of our individual lives.

People like this transcend the mundane world while still including it in all its diversity, richness, and nitty-grittiness. They tend to see God in *each other and in every person they meet, even while dealing with a very human personality with its various quirks and foibles. They draw forth the wholeness of the person, whether their own child, a relative, or a friend, neighbor, or associate. They truly make life interesting, enjoyable, and rewarding in its exchanges.*

Another family lives in much the same way, welcoming, honoring, and nurturing the wholeness of each of their children. I have been at the last three births of their family of five.

Deidre has a wonderful ability to dive into the depths of giving birth, of mothering, of nurturing, and of being wife in an ever-delightful unfolding of relationship. Her labors have been long; they have been incredibly short. (I nearly missed the second one I attended because I stopped at the store at her request to bring them a few supplies they had not gotten yet!) Regardless of the type of labor, she has, without a doubt, trusted the process and trusted her body, trusted her support system and trusted her caregivers. She has no desire to hold back from life or birth or pain or joy. She simply rests as fully and completely as she can in each moment of her experience. Her way of interacting with life comes from that place deep inside where truth, purity, and lack of guile rest.

They have chosen a lifestyle that differs a great deal from the mainstream of our society, living on a beautiful piece of land at the edge of a small village without television or the latest in modern conveniences. She stays home with her children, home schooling and providing them with a rich source of opportunities. Both of these parents being very intelligent, they discuss openly with their children the dilemmas and challenges they face in choosing to live this way. They share their philosophies of life and challenge their children to be socially conscious. Their children are some of the best behaved, well adjusted, interactive, and emotionally stable of any kids I know.

This birth brought the acknowledging of our challenges and responsibilities of life. It has broadened and deepened our perspectives on the meaning of life and being strong in the face of sometimes difficult decisions. For me personally, it has been an opportunity to simply observe and be with, to the best of my ability, some of the more contracted and closed off places in my way of relating both to myself and to the people close to me. It has been one of my tendencies to hold back from life, to not acknowledge something uncomfortable, to deny the possibility that life may not be "perfect."

Deidre had been very, very ill several weeks prior to her birth with a virus that passed from child to child and parent to parent. Recovering from this took time, but she felt well once again by the time she gave birth. When her baby was born with the coming of the sun over the distant hill, I was filled with anxiety and worry because the responses of this newborn to life and to breastfeeding and stimulation seemed so different from her other children's. On each of my visits after the birth, I would be filled with concern and yet not be able to confront my concerns directly. I focused on how the feedings were going, the number of wet diapers and stools, sleep cycles and interactions, crying or not, everything but my real concerns. I sought for reassurance that this baby was normal and would be okay, that this family would not have to face any pain, which I would not have to grieve once again. Two weeks went by while I walked through the "valley of the shadow of death," a place that was hauntingly familiar to me.

Memories overwhelmed me and I could do nothing but turn around and look to where I had been in days gone by but not forgotten, days and nights that will never be forgotten in my heart and soul. I had lived much of my life with the view that not only could I ease or erase the pain and suffering of my own life, but it was my mission in life to ease or erase the pain of everyone I came into contact with in my life. I thought I could reach the state of perpetual happiness by my will alone. I was, therefore, shocked to the root of my existence when, in my mid-twenties, my second child was diagnosed with cerebral palsy, a type of brain damage that affected the use of his muscles to varying degrees.

I remember only seven days of lying on the living room couch barely able to care for my two young sons as I fought the demons of fate. Vivid in my memory at that time was an experience in the delivery room as a nurse three years previously, when a physician had stated that this woman who was just about to give birth had a child with cerebral palsy. A sudden bolt of lightening had gone through me from the top of my head down through my feet. Time was suspended for those few moments, and I "knew' that I would have a child with cerebral palsy. I had, either fortunately or unfortunately, forgotten that moment until I heard the words now as a diagnosis for my son.

After battling those seven days with the demons of fairness, with whim, with why-me, with why-him, I finally emerged into a place of relative acceptance. It was a lonely, forlorn path to tread, one that seemingly nothing in my life had prepared me to face and endure. Acceptance in those following weeks and months was still a bitter pill to swallow as the realities of the situation began to emerge. The questions continued even as I began making the adjustments so necessary to incorporating this into our lives. Where was the God who could let such a terrible thing happen to an innocent child? Who was that God? What was my relationship to Him? How could I ever trust life again? I could find nothing and no one to support me in my pain. I could only see reflections around me of people who sneered, who stared, who made cruel remarks, who blamed me. Not only was I aware of my own pain, but I was aware of the struggles my son, and later my daughter, also diagnosed, would have to make to carve out a place for themselves in life and in a culture that was particularly unforgiving in many ways. I could love them with all of my heart, but I had to come to terms with the fact that I could not give them what they could not find for themselves.

These memories reminded me of the denial I had clung to, the fear of accepting what my heart knew to be the truth, and the turning away from the wounding to my heart that only a mother can know. I remembered the long process of coming to a place of unconditional love and peace, and being able to accept both for myself and for them that they must face their own personal struggles that cannot help but be colored by their unique history and circumstances. I remembered the pain of facing the diagnosis for myself, and then facing the rest of the world with commitment and strength that I would do everything in my power to support and protect them.

And then I remembered the birth of my last child, born at twenty-six weeks. It was he who brought home to my still-struggling heart and soul an unconditional love and acceptance of life.

During the week he clung to life, I lived a lifetime, it seemed. I struggled and fought once again with the unfairness, the fear, the longing, the heart-wrenching ache, and the endless possibilities of what his life might mean to him, to me, to his siblings, and to us as a family. The night before he died, I finally felt peace descend and fill my heart like a soothing balm. My heart and soul were full, and I only knew that I loved him profoundly and unconditionally, and I would love him regardless of any handicaps, be they physical, mental, or both. I would accept fully the will of God. I was past trying to make "deals" with God.

It was as if he was waiting for me to come to that place—of realizing the blessings he brought with him—before he left this world. The grief, which lingers even after so many years can never dim the gift of his life, the gift of surrender, love, and acceptance, always to be an elixir of balm to an aching heart. He lives forever in a place of peace and oneness deep inside me.

I remembered all of this and more as I lived a life between worlds, my world of the past and my world of the present in relationship with this family. I watched myself keep trying to make things "right" inside myself so that I wouldn't have to say dreadful words out loud. I went to sleep one night with a prayer in my heart to God that if things were fine and I was overreacting to my own painful past, to please let me know in a way that I couldn't miss, the proverbial neon sign! When I awoke in the morning, I simply knew I had to call. I could no longer hide behind my usual defenses, my habitual patterns of denial, of not wanting any confrontation, of not wanting to take risks and later find myself wrong, humiliated, and feeling foolish. I could not longer focus on playing it safe and not delivering words that might hurt or wound or anger.

And so it was that I made that call to express my concerns, my inner feelings, and my wish to communicate my concerns in a way that honored but did not wound. I simply wanted to open the doors to discussion and possible action, but did not want to demand or control or blame or shame anyone, myself included. The words were not met with equal concern, and I felt like I had stepped through a huge doorway that had blocked my own acceptance of life as it came regardless of whether I deemed it good or bad, right or wrong, painful or pleasant. It had taken courage in spite of the depth of the relationship we had. I was going against "my own grain" in doing things a different way.

The ending to this story has even more magic and mystery to relate. Over the next several years, this baby's development concerned family and friends and there were many questions. The family pulled together and offered this little one complete love and acceptance, while having absolute faith and conviction that he would come into his full state of being in his own time. They stimulated, played with, loved, cherished, and challenged him in honest, open, and loving ways. And now, two years later, he has caught up and surpassed his siblings. Gone are the questions and the doubts. The truth is that it didn't ultimately matter in the ways that really count. Love and acceptance of life in this family is total; nothing is held back. Labels aren't needed or wanted or useful. Their paradigm for family means that every child is seen in his or her wholeness, making it easy to provide the challenges needed for growth and to give genuine support and recognition of where each one excels. The range of normal dissolves into allowing each person to be multidimensional and whole. Divine meets divine; sacred meets sacred; life meets life; and love dissolves into love. What more is there, ever? I truly believe that the faith of this family overcame what might have been an entirely different outcome had they chosen to put their belief in labels or in the doubting of others. It is a miracle.

I'm reminded of another quote by Deepak Chopra in the book *Journey into Healing*. It goes like this . . .

Accept what comes to you totally and completely so that you can appreciate it, learn from it, and then let it go.

Another experience that comes to mind was extremely painful for everyone involved, but it, too, is a story full of grace and faith and acceptance even in the midst of tragedy and heartache. This couple was having their first baby together. Their view of life came from a strong Eastern religious tradition, and they attempted to live according to this philosophy in their everyday lives. The bond between this woman and me was strong and deep right from our initial contact over the phone. It intensified throughout the pregnancy, allowing both of us to move through some past traumas as we shared on deeper and deeper levels.

Tragedy struck in labor. The baby's heartbeat dropped, recovered, and dropped again a short time later. We left for the hospital several blocks away immediately. "A sense of calm and peace descended" upon the mother as we arrived at the hospital. Ironically, as we walked in, I could only remember my rather impassioned plea a week earlier that the hospital could be the best place to have a baby in light of the fact that she was overdue. The next hour was a blur as she was admitted and subsequently taken to the surgery room for an emergency cesarean. A steady albeit low heart rate of the baby dropped precipitously as the bed literally passed through the surgery doors. The baby was stillborn.

We held this child afterward, each of us crying torrents of tears of sadness and grief and loss. I was suddenly filled with a sense that midwifery works both ways, one way as the soul makes its way into the worldly body and the other through the gates of eternity as it returns to its real home. While I felt like we were trapped in a nightmare with no way out, and I wanted nothing more than to turn the hands of the clock backward in time, I also was aware that I was being given an opportunity to midwife this soul through its last journey. Can I ever know if the truth was revealed accurately in those moments? I doubt it. And yet some grain of truth has touched my heart and changed my life, as well as my knowledge of what we are about, of what life is about below the surface of our immediate awareness.

These people grieved for the child they would never come to know and would not see grow through the years of infancy and childhood on into adulthood. They grieved for their lost parenthood, and they grieved for the pain that their family and loved ones suffered. They grieved for my suffering as I grieved for theirs. And yet, as they made this journey through the weeks turned months turned years, there was no bitterness, no blame, no recrimination, no struggle against what had been and what was. I watched resistance to life dissolve into the welcoming of their open arms as they embraced their pain and worldly suffering, and the beliefs that there was a reason and that everything is a lesson in life. Another quote from Deepak Chopra explains the state of being that they lived by throughout this ordeal. "When you resist the flow of life, you are actually resisting your own inner nature, for everything that happens to us is a reflection of who we are." It was one of the most vivid examples of acceptance in life and in death, and of extracting blessings from all situations, that I have ever seen.

As difficult as that experience was for me, because I did have remorse, self-blame, bitterness, and judgment, I came to see that life and lessons and blessings come not in the forms we expect or desire, but in entirely different forms. Death is a part of life; suffering is a part of life. We have a choice not in what comes to us but in how we respond to it, relate to it, and step into our future with it. Pema Chodron in When Things Fall Apart: Heart Advice for Difficult Times speaks of this:

> *When we find ourselves in a mess, we don't have to feel guilty about it. Instead, we could reflect on the fact that how we relate to this mess will be sowing the seeds of how we will relate to whatever happens next. We can make ourselves miserable, or we can make ourselves strong. The amount of effort is the same. Right now we are creating our state of mind for tomorrow, not to mention this afternoon, next week, next year, and all the years of our lives.*

Blessings, I am learning, are often veiled and hidden in life's most challenging aspects. As time advances, I am learning more and more to "let go and let God," and to feel gratitude in my heart for situations and encounters that leave me sometimes bloodied and wounded on the side of the path. God leans down in some unsuspecting moment to lift aside the veil that prevents me from seeing the truth, beauty, joy, and love that rest in my own sense of fullness. I can only surrender in that moment to a truth greater than my previous understanding. As I step back and continue to "midwife" my children silently even in their adulthood as they make their own way through life, I find myself with the urge to midwife myself as I enter another phase of a life that seems to be both winding down and speeding up. And I can only thank God for having shown me so much through so many others and for continuing to do so. It is such a sacred and holy path.

Being "midwife" to those close to me, whether friend, relative, child, or associate, is not always easy; in fact, it is much harder in most ways because of the needs, old patterns, desires, anger, and frustration that can build up over years of interactions. I find myself calling on God even more as I seek to provide the immense space for those close to me to find their own freedom—from expectations, from cultural norms, from outdated family dynamics, or even from any ideas of what might be good for them in my limited perspective. They don't necessarily appreciate my stance or my way of being, I have found, but I can only continue to trust in the intuitive direction I am being shown, in the same way that I have learned to trust that unseen, directive quality in birth. I am learning to accept life as it comes regardless of whether it meets with my approval or not. Life, I frequently remind myself, is full of blessings when it is seen as a process of continual learning, continual balancing, and continual shifting into greater awareness and ability to follow through, so that the blessings have room to appear and grow and shape a new me, a new you.

In this chapter, I have focused on loss in one form or another a great deal. Although loss is a difficult thing to reconcile on many levels, it actually takes incredible strength and courage in any situation to be able to accept the will of God. This includes when good things happen in life, all the times things work out the way we want, or we are saved from suffering by a stroke of luck or the generosity of another. Loss is difficult to accept, but sometimes we have as much difficulty accepting the easy, fun, joyful, thrilling moments that touch our hearts with such abundance, because we are much more familiar with suffering, or because we are touched by a feeling of unworthiness, thinking we don't deserve wonderful things to happen when those we love might be suffering or struggling. Regardless, at some point in this process of accepting life as a blessing, we find ourselves connecting to the larger human life which is full of pain, glory, success, and failure, and of being "in the flow" or "going against the flow."

One final sharing explores this connection, this awareness of all lives and all experiences that is brought out by the painful losses we each have at some point in our journey.

> *I am turning once again to face the grief/loss. I basically degenerated into a feeling of utterly despairing depression, certain I'd failed as a woman, lost my chance at another baby, and that the only thing left for me was duty to [my first child] and the great joy of her love. Without her, I can't imagine the depression. How do women survive? Until this happened to me, I had no conception, no idea what women bear. I've met mothers who lost their firstborn after full term plus 48 hours; 3 moths; 15 years. What does time matter? We'll always miss our babies. . . . I must do some grief processing. I know I want another baby, God willing. But I must let go of this spirit. It's a pain. . . . I just wanted to express my gratitude to you, your profession, and all of the amazing women who have suffered and lost so very much. They continue bravely as must I. . . .*

Chapter Nine
Humility and Joy

In the eyes of an innocent orphan child
    And the wizened eyes of an old beggar . . .
In the eyes of a hungry street urchin
    And the eyes of an aged wrinkled grandmother . . .
In the eyes of a gentle homeless puppy
    And the eyes of a painted temple deity . . .
In the eyes of a sari-draped bride
    And the eyes of a maroon-robed monk . . .
In the eyes of a dying newborn baby
        And the closed eyes of a shrouded body at the burning ghat . . .
In the eyes of a devout Tibetan pilgrim
    And the loving eyes of a handicapped boy . . .
In the eyes of a beautiful turquoise-adorned Tibetan nomad
     And the eyes of a selfless Catholic nun . . .
In the eyes of the temple's golden Buddha
    And in the eyes of my sweet, sweet love . . .
In the eyes of faithful friends
    And in the eyes of curious strangers . . .
In the eyes of my Guru's picture
    And the eyes of the most holy Rinpoche . . .
And finally . . .
    In the eyes of my own mirror . . .

In the deep, deep silence
    Of the vast stillness of my own heart . . .
I saw God.
    And my eyes are wet with streaming tears . . .
In so many eyes, in so many forms

It is ALL ONE, the living presence of Truth . . .
And I am blessed and I am humbled by such a vision
To dwell, even for a moment, in such sacred company
With the Lord.

27 January 1997, my journal Kathmandu

Humility and joy. Why, you might ask, do I include them together? A moment in time stands out in my memory: at the moment of a birth, as we stood gazing at the top of the baby's head, a dad spoke words that still remain with me. It had been a difficult labor, a long, hard labor that had used up all of our resources, physical and psychological and emotional. We were each exhausted in our own way. An early spring storm full of blustery winds, freezing rain and snow had hurled against the frozen windows as mom attempted to push this baby out at home. Unsuccessful in her attempts, we endured a harrowing drive to the hospital with the storm continuing its unrelenting attack. Within a short time, we were in the delivery room watching the baby's head emerge. The dad looked from the baby's head into my face and said, **"This is the first time I've seen you smile all night. Your face is full of joy."**

My awareness stopped in that moment, drawn to my own experience within me. I realized then and there how this moment of birth stops me every time, filling my heart and soul with profound delight and joy. And in that realization came humility as I saw how truly blessed I am to share in this miracle time after time and how truly happy it makes me. At the moment of birth, I go beyond any circumstances which may have led to this moment into a beautiful place of greeting and welcoming the coming child. It never fails to touch my soul or put that smile on my face. There are times when tears fall as I respond to the welcoming of the child by the family.

Jean Shinoda Bolen speaks of joy and grace as coming together in the form of a synchronistic even in *The Tao of Psychology.*

> **Joy is the emotion that the artist, theoretician, or inventor experiences at the moment of creation. Joy accompanies anything transcendent in which the ego experiences something greater than itself. Joy is the mood whenever something 'new' is brought into being. It is present with a heightened awareness of actualizing one's potentialities**

and always accompanies an intuitively felt Tao experience.

Humility seems to arrive by some sort of unexplainable process that I identify as Grace during those special kinds of moments in my life. In these moments, I come to realize the gift and preciousness of human life and the human condition. I see how deeply connected we are to one another, and much of the surface tensions, thoughts, and judgments fall away to leave only the essence. I am left sharing a truly intimate and magical moment with another human being. In *A Path With Heart*, Jack Kornfield reminds us that it is from this act of being touched by the world deep within our hearts that we have the opportunity to connect to the peace that lies underneath our lives, the place of "peace that passeth all understanding."

> *As we allow the world to touch us deeply, we recognize that just as there is pain in our own lives, so there is pain in everyone else's life. This is the birth of wise understanding. Wise understanding sees that suffering is inevitable, that all things are born to die. Wise understanding sees and accepts life as a whole. With wise understanding we allow ourselves to contain all things, both dark and light, and we come to a sense of peace. This is not the peace of denial or running away, but the peace we find in the heart that has rejected nothing, that touches all things with compassion.*

Compassion is a quality that I have found I need for myself just as much as others need it from me. Being self-critical does not allow a lot of room for the truth to present itself gently or clearly. It seems that we sometimes do not see ourselves as others see us. It's not so much that we are right and "they" are wrong, or that "they" are right and we are wrong. It's more that as we begin to clean the mirror of our own image and see more of the truth, we reach a middle ground where we can lighten up, step back, and begin to appreciate how we do touch the lives and hearts of those around us.

One of the greatest lessons of my life has come from someone who started out as a client and then moved into becoming my apprentice for several years. She became a great friend and support person as I moved to touch other, deeper aspects of myself. The midwife in me was transformed by this ongoing, deeply bonding interaction. In her words, she shares the experience as it was for her and as it continued to be long after her very precious daughter was born.

Thanks. I love having you as my mentor. You're a wonderful combination of magic and spirit balanced with earthiness. I remember the first time you came out to the house. There's nothing specific that you said or did but [my husband] and I finally began feeling comfortable with having a home birth. Our first few visits we kept at that safe distance but then little by little you began showing yourself to me and little by little I began to trust you, not just as a midwife but as someone very real, someone who wouldn't judge me by my housekeeping abilities, someone who wouldn't be disappointed if I whined during my birth, someone I could be real with. As we continued to open up to each other I began to realize that I could give up having to control the birth. What a relief it was to finally be able to trust the process to unfold as it should and to know you would react to that unfolding in whatever way was appropriate.

I am so grateful that you have continued to be my teacher. Whenever I am around you as you work, I am in total awe of your ability to balance your intelligence and experience with your intuition and kindness.

And right now as all the self-doubts and regrets are trying to take over, you have given me the gift of <u>our</u> birth story, reminding me of my woman strength, of light. Thank you.

These words were written quite some time after her birth and well into her apprenticeship. The gift she gave me as an apprentice was her devotion, her willingness to be present, to absorb what was happening, and to honor each and every experience. The gift she gave me as a client was a profound level of trust and acceptance of me as a person and as a midwife. Her pregnancy was a long journey into the depths of her soul, and her birth was a short-in-clock-hours journey into the magic and mystery of motherhood. She taught me humility and showed me the joy of passing on my skills and knowledge to a successor. She showed me that joy is experienced most vividly when I am being real. It doesn't mean only being joyful when things are going well, just like I want them to be. It doesn't mean not experiencing joy when things are not going the way I want them to. It simply means being with everything that is in my world in the moment and being aware of my "realness" while touching the deeper, more sacred magic that underlies that state. Mindfulness becomes the gift as well as the way to receive the gift.

In *Sacred World*, Jeremy Hayward says that:

> *when we see that others feel the same way, it breaks our hearts. From broken hearts, our hearts of sadness and longing and joy, we can look at others and feel their heart of sadness and longing and goodness. Then we feel our direct connection with them. We feel that their heart is our heart, that there is really no difference between their longing and our longing.*

He continues to speak of the desire to share our joy with others.

> *The only way you can share your joy is through your presence and your relationships, through communication of your genuine connection with others.*

Ironically, it has often been the fathers of these babies who have touched my heart with the realization that humility and joy go hand in hand. They have such a different perspective on birthing, a perspective that is poignant and respectful and sometimes humorous, with the bit of distance that they have as watchers and witnesses to this amazing process. Here are the words of one father.

> *[She] hates hospital food so we opted for a home birth. The hot tub was a lifesaver. It really helped those mean contractions. However, down the home stretch even the comforting bubbles couldn't quiet the birthing beast. Out of her petite lungs came the sound of monsters. The neighbors must have thought we were harpooning whales on the deck. [The baby's] delivery at home was much easier than . . . in the hospital. There was nobody messing with us in our bedroom. The midwife let out a few cheers, [my wife] let out a few screams—and before I knew it I was holding [our baby].*

The next letter shows how much more relaxed he was at the second experience of birthing at home, the "old pro" aspect comes alive.

Life could not be sweeter. The beautiful but modest baby . . . has already won us over. She sleeps more than an old dog and cries only when it is absolutely necessary. [Her] birth was just what the doctor ordered, but without the doctor. For the second time, we decided to have a "home birth." There are no physicians meddling in the natural progression of things and it also gives [my wife] a chance to feel macho. The "little woman" woke up at 2 A.M. . . . and said "something is going on down there. . . ." By 5 A.M. it became obvious that I should boil some water and rip up some old undies . . . we had a baby coming our way. The midwife got to our place by 6 A.M. By then [we] were in the hot tub trying to boil away her discomfort. Soon it was up to our bedroom where the pace picked up considerably. This time, instead of sounding like a whale being harpooned, [she] sang during the most severe contractions. It was a little like opera, but with a more urgent quality. . . . Together we all watched as a 7 pound, 14 ounce girl, about 21 inches long, left her old world and joined us in what we now believe will be a better world. . . .

The following article. which was written by a husband and father I thoroughly enjoyed, is taken from a local publication a few years ago. This father has a unique perspective that he was willing to share with us. His words are eloquent and descriptive of the process he participated in with such relish.

A Father, A Mother and Four Midwives
One man's view of childbirth
The beginning of life is an electric experience. Everyone and everything changes. For me, my fatherhood began the day my wife found out that she was pregnant. From then on our lives were different. Thank God we were given nine months to prepare for the birth. We didn't need that much time to set up the crib or even to choose names – we needed the time to define our lives. [My wife] was no longer to be just my wife, or my best friend, but she was becoming the mother of my children. I had always wanted to be a father, and we planned our pregnancy, so I thought I was ready.

But what a thrill to think about having our own baby. During that first pregnancy nothing else mattered as much as preparing for the birth.

[My wife] researched everything she could find on pregnancy and childbirth. She read books over and over, as if she were studying for an exam. I told her I had never seen her more excited about anything. She laughed that most people spend more time researching the purchase of a new VCR than they do preparing for a new baby. We both wanted only the best. Of course, we didn't know what that meant, but we were committed to finding out. [She] called the local maternity center, a small facility run by Certified Nurse Midwives (CNMs), and scheduled us for a tour. I don't think I had ever heard of a midwife. Over the next ten years, four midwives would guide us through the births of our children.

Marty

The first midwife we met was Marty. She was a young CNM who had already assisted in hundreds of births. Her attitude was so upbeat and enthusiastic it seemed like we were at a prep rally. She showed us the maternity center, always describing birth as a wonderful experience. Marty later taught our weekly childbirth preparation classes where we learned above all else that the responsibility for the healthy birth of our children is ours. So many people seem to rely blindly on others to control their pregnancies. Marty gave us the encouragement and education to help us take the lead. Each week we looked forward to Marty's class. We became close friends with the other first-time parents and began to think of ourselves that way.

One night during our class a woman was in labor in another room. We could hear her contraction moans, so Marty took the opportunity to describe the stages of her labor. This laboring mother's attitude about birth was so open and honest that she invited us into the room so she could describe her feelings during the contractions. You don't ever forget a lesson taught with that kind of visual aid.

Marty wasn't able to be at our first birth, but she was at our second, and will always be a precious friend. She gave us the most important gift of all—our own self-confidence.

Alex

Alex was our midwife at the birth of our first child. Like Marty, she was young and positive. But she had a sharp sense of humor, and a very matter-of-fact personality. She was the one who first let us hear our daughter's heartbeat, who measured and charted [my wife's] progress, who gave advice about diet and preparing for the big day. As our due date approached, Alex told [my wife] the best way to get labor started was to walk—a lot. So [we] walked everywhere, on some nights to the top of twelve story buildings. It didn't get the labor started, but we both had great thigh muscles for months after.

The morning of the day our daughter was born, Alex made us comfortable and gave us a pep talk. She checked us periodically, but, mostly let us have the time to ourselves which is just what we needed. It is that sensitivity to parents that we found common in all of our midwives. When it came time for the birth Alex was ready, and [my wife] did great. [Our daughter] came out with her eyes open wide— looking for Mom. Alex made sure everyone was fine, got [the new mom] something healthy to eat and then went to rugby practice.

Sandy

After our first birth, there was no doubt that we would have a nurse midwife at the delivery of all of our children. The maternity center had closed since our first birth so we decided to have our second baby at home. We found Sandy, a midwife who did home births. She was a quiet woman who let us do the talking. Rather than give stock answers, she let us think our questions through. This pregnancy was like a dream—no problems, no worries. During labor Sandy knitted a little stocking cap for the baby. Marty came to help Sandy at the birth, but they both let [my wife] run the show. She decided what, when and where. But I wanted to do more—so they stood back as [she] pushed, as I eased my first son into the world.

Karen

Our third child was also born at home with the help of our last midwife, Karen. Remarkably, she is the only midwife of the four to have her own children. And as with all of them, her love of children was clear in her eyes. She made us feel very relaxed on her visits. When the time came Karen warned us that this birth might be fast. I ran hot water in the sink and then ran back to catch [the baby]. We just laughed as we took turns holding him. It was two hours before we realized the water was still running in the sink. Throughout the pregnancy Karen had been there whenever we needed her, but never got in the way.

These four midwives, Marty, Alex, Sandy and Karen, seem like big sisters to me now—part of our family. In my life there have been a handful of people that made a lasting impression—my parents, certain teachers, a coach, my wife—and my midwives. Life and the beginning of life wouldn't be the same without them.

Sometimes we are called to be midwife to the midwife in both subtle and not-so-subtle ways. It can be for an actual birth, as many of the midwives in this service have given birth at home with their fellow midwives in attendance both in supportive roles and in traditional midwifery roles. Performing this role works both ways since life is always about learning and being the student and then turning around and sharing it with another. One may be midwife at one time and then recipient of that guidance the next time.

One of the most enriching, expanding, and rewarding experiences of my life came from a fellow midwife and friend of many years. She asked me to read a poem for her and her bridegroom at their wedding called the *Tao of Marriage*. Being reluctant if not downright terrified of public speaking brought me up against many of my fears: fear of failure, fear of making a mistake, fear of doing it wrong, and fear of her not receiving the purity of my love and the honoring of their marriage.

Well, I practiced the poem for weeks, memorizing it by speaking it in front of my mirror, in my car, in the tub, while doing dishes. I prayed for Grace and found the space in my heart where this was no longer about me or how I did but only about the heart-felt love and blessings that I wished to give her and her husband. I felt shaky inside and my legs literally trembled on my seldom-worn high-heeled shoes, but my voice was strong and I could feel grace flow through me. I felt that in this simple request, she had become my midwife; by her faith and trust in me, she had pulled my hesitancy out into the open where I could deal with it straightforwardly. And, in turn, it became my own strength and the glory of my own heartbeat in my ears. I could see also that we have been co-midwives to each other in many ways and at many times in our relationship. I watch as she continues to grow and evolve and mature as a midwife, a woman, a wife, and a soul. And I can see how it is these kinds of bonds that nourish each other and provide support and encouragement along the way. These are some of the words she spoke after her wedding.

> *I know we don't see each other much, but I want you to know I've learned so much from you over the years about love and compassion and patience. You taught me—years ago—the most important things I know about what it means to be a midwife. I'm honored to know you and it was truly a blessing to have you be a part of our wedding. . . .*

Another midwife was "midwife" to me after the birth of the stillborn (previous chapter), and I was terrified of doing any more births, either at home or in the hospital. She had had a similar thing happen in her practice years ago and so could truly understand and be with me during this grieving process. She listened. She shared. She supported. And she promised to come in for as many births as it took me to feel confident and comfortable once again. For once in my life, I let people support me. She came in for one birth and sat quietly in the corner. She came in again for a second birth and stayed out at the nurses' station. The third time I called her and she stayed at home. That was all it took. I felt the support; I knew I could call her (which I occasionally did over the years with the homebirth practice). And so I picked up the pieces and went on with my life and my career and on with the grieving without letting it overwhelm me and destroy my ability to do what I had been trained to do. That kind of support is the healer as it leads us to our own inner awareness and strength. Deepak Chopra, in *Journey into Healing,* says:

> *Our pure awareness is already whole, already healed. If we feel divided inside, the solution is to bring ourselves back to wholeness. Consciousness is its own healer.*

Friends like these who take on the role of midwife can show us the *real us,* thereby giving the gift of making us whole and complete within.

Chapter Ten
Faith

"Faith," she answered in response to my question. "I focused on being calm and on waiting. I prayed for you to drive safely and for you to arrive in time for the birth. I never ever doubted for a moment. . . . I knew you would get here in time and that you would be safe.

F aith comes in many shapes, colors, and forms, and out of many traditions and cultures, but in its essence, it is the same wherever it is found in its truest and more pure state. I have witnessed faith expressed by those whose paths have led to Christianity, Buddhism, Judaism, Islamic traditions, Native American ways, and New Age philosophies, and in more simple beliefs in life itself with no specific name or form. I have witnessed miracles that come from the depths of surrender to this belief in a Higher Power or Consciousness, in God with many names, in Spirit manifest, in Buddha-nature. Faith supports this willingness to surrender and to trust in the process of life and all that it brings us through our daily experiences. It is truly the foundation from which all other attributes emerge. It makes possible a sense of adventure, and allows one to be steady in the witness consciousness, giving one's living the strength and clarity it needs. It is the foundation for integrity and fearlessness and allowing all blessings to flow. It allows for patience, the state of things unfolding and blossoming in their own time and their own way. And it allows for gentleness and loving-kindness.

There are three births that I would like to share, each one very different and yet all connected by the link of an unshakable and deeply abiding faith expressed in unique and individual ways.

The first story relates to the words shared at the beginning of this chapter. Melinda was a young woman having her second baby. I had attended her first birth, and it had gone easily and quickly, a fact she attributed to her faith that that birth was as God had intended. A convert to her husband's religion, she displayed a deep sense of conviction in its tenets. The complicating factor in this pregnancy had nothing to do with her state of health but with the fact that she had moved three hours away to a place with no nurse midwives practicing in the home setting, the place where she was strongly committed to birthing once again. We agreed that she would come back to the city and stay with friends from the time she started her thirty-seventh week of pregnancy to await the birth. She was understandably reluctant to do this but agreed to it because I felt so strongly that it was the wisest and safest of the possible alternatives.

Because of her rapid first birth, I cautioned her to call at the first signs of any change that might be indicative of labor, and to be prepared to go to the hospital if she didn't think she could make the three-hour journey. The day prior to thirty-seven weeks and her planned departure for the city, she called with what at first seemed like an early sign of change. Upon further questioning, however, it became apparent that it was much more than an early sign in her case and that the changes had started the prior evening. I truly felt that she was in active labor and there was little, if any, chance of either one of us making the trip in time for the birth.

To make a long story much shorter, she was absolutely convinced that I had time to make the trip before she gave birth. In the long pause over the phone line that ensued, I distinctly heard a voice echo inside me saying "go," simple and straight to the point. I actually argued with the voice in my head as well as the one on the other end of the phone but to no avail. Neither was having any of my objections or rationalizations or alternative suggestions. The word "go" simply repeated itself more loudly this time. Now, I am not much in the habit of hearing literal voices nor do I usually allow it to rule over my logical mind in times like this, but there seemed to be no going against the voice, the command, that I let go and trust. The trusting seemed to be about knowing that this was, indeed, what I was supposed to be doing regardless of the outcome. I told Melinda to lie down and call 911 or to go to the hospital if she thought the baby was going to come prior to my arrival.

Needless to say, I spent the next three hours going through every possible scenario imaginable, praying to God to be with her and with me, and to let this baby be born safely under whatever circumstances were most beneficial. My ego was reduced to a slobbering, fear-based concept. I stopped at one point en route to call her from a pay phone. Her words were both reassuring and aimed at supporting me, telling me to drive carefully and to stay safe. She felt fine, she said, and was lying down and nothing had changed from the time of our previous conversation. I reiterated my instructions. Somewhat reassured and calmed, I finally let go and surrendered to God's will, trusting that neither Melinda nor I would be required to endure anything but the will of God. Peace filled my heart, and I felt freer and steadier than I ever would have believed possible.

Arriving at her home, I was prepared to be with the situation fully whether I found her attended by emergency rescue, gone to the hospital, delivered by herself, or still waiting for my arrival undelivered. She had her first "hard, pushing contraction," in fact, just as I drove up in front of her house. This healthy baby girl was born several minutes later into the gentle, loving, waiting hands of her mother and her breathless midwife.

"Faith," she answered in response to my question of how she had managed to not give birth knowing she was "ready" at least forty-five minutes prior to my arrival. "I focused on being calm and on waiting. I prayed for you to drive safely and to arrive in time for the birth. I never ever doubted. . . . I knew you would get here in time for the birth and that you would be safe. I put it all into God's hands and I just laid here quietly waiting.

I was humbled. I knew that grace had visited us all that day and that I had personally been given a glimpse of what miracles are available to those whose faith is strong and unshakable.

The second experience occurred during a pregnancy. It remains to this day in my mind and heart the most significant and visible proof that miracles do happen in today's modern world. God is alive and at work this very moment. The memory of this time still brings tears to my eyes just as it did then. Kathy (see chapter 8) was in her fourth month of pregnancy with her seventh child when she developed a respiratory infection that progressed to pneumonia. On bed rest, antibiotics, and a cough suppressant, she was still racked by bouts of intense coughing that possibly contributed to a spontaneous and premature rupture of her membranes, the bag of water surrounding the fetus. She called me to confirm her suspicions, which I did. After consulting with a physician, she was given the options of an assisted termination, waiting for labor to begin, or waiting in the extremely unlikely event that the membranes might reseal themselves. This was deemed unlikely because of the copious amount of amniotic fluid she was leaking.

While stunned by this turn of events, they prayed fervently and felt at ease to simply wait and see what would happen, God's will be done. She continued her antibiotics, bed rest, and cough suppressant while monitoring her temperature frequently. Keeping in close contact, I knew that she would periodically begin to have contractions and cramping, feel increased pelvic pressure and lose more amniotic fluid. Then all of the symptoms would subside for some time, only to repeat the sequence once again. This took place over the next ten days to two weeks. She continued the bed rest and the treatment for the pneumonia while also dealing with all of the emotional fluctuations brought about by the uncertainty of the outcome.

*While lying on the couch one afternoon, she was prompted by an inner urging to listen to the radio, a religious station managed by her husband. A song immediately began to play that included words to the effect that . . . **though the waters be parted, God will finish what He has started** (paraphrase), and she was filled with the Grace of knowing that this pregnancy would continue as God had, indeed, intended. She stopped leaking fluid over the next several hours. Calling and sharing this with me, I felt the goose bumps rise and tears fill my eyes as I knew that God had spoken to her with absolute clarity and reassurance. The truth had been revealed through that intuitive guidance that speaks to the depth of her faith—the faith of all the family, in fact—in God, in the process of birth, and in life itself.*

The pregnancy did continue quite normally, and she gave birth to a healthy and vigorous baby boy a few days after her due date to the profound gratitude and rejoicing of everyone who knew what this pregnancy had entailed. A miracle had happened as far as we were concerned, and I had been blessed by being a witness to it and a participant in it.

A great Master has said that faith is like a magnet that pulls God toward us. I love this image. Just as in the birth story above, these words were true at Charlene's birth.

Having her sixth child, Charlene was the epitome of calmness and acceptance. She wanted to experience this last birth in the privacy of her home. Her husband agreed somewhat reluctantly but with a natural faith in life. As it came to pass, they were moving out of state right after school was out for the summer, the exact time that this child was due.

Talking the night before the planned departure, we said our farewells, and I wished them the best of luck. Nothing was happening in terms of any labor, and they were finally packed and ready to leave at dawn. Having always had some early warning of impending labor with each of her births, we reflected on God's timing but we were, nonetheless, sad. I mentally wished them well as I awoke at first light the next morning, never imagining what was to unfold with the coming of the day.

Midmorning I received a call from her. The very moment she had gotten into the truck and fastened her seat belt, she had felt her first labor contraction. They had been hanging out since then to see if it was, in fact, labor and would continue. I was two hours away from this woman but agreed to come immediately to determine if it was actually labor. I did, and it was.

The labor progressed normally until the end, when she began to bleed. There was no time to consider a transport and due to the circumstances, I had no trained assistant with me, only a layperson. I prayed fervently to God to be with me and to guide me and to ensure that this mom and this baby would be safe. I prayed for help from the core of my soul. As I took a deep breath and looked up to give a command to one of her friends that I knew could cope in an emergency, a young woman in a nursing uniform walked through the bedroom door. She was a neighbor and a new labor and delivery nurse in training, just arriving home after her shift. She had never been in this particular situation before, but she remained calm and readily followed my instructions. The baby was born safely and expeditiously into a welcoming family a few moments later, the placenta was delivered, and the bleeding was controlled, all of which the mom tolerated well.

It was then that I knew God had answered my prayer without hesitation. An angel in white had appeared to give us the help we needed. I was filled with gratitude and awe as well as a sense of no longer being alone in my life.

Faith is something that has deepened within me over time, through experiences such as these that I have shared, as well as others with less drama or intensity but with no less power. Birth seems to have given faith a home within me where it resides, grows, and expands; and that faith then emerges into all other aspects of my life. Faith, for me, has led the way to a higher level of fearlessness and trust—in myself, in the Lord, in life itself, and in knowing that everything does happen for the best when I have surrendered enough. It has led me to deepen my search for the truth inside my own heart.

About eight years ago, a set of circumstances led me to attend a firewalking ceremony. For those of you who may not know of this tradition, a fire is allowed to burn down until nothing is left but red-hot, smoldering coals. The ritual leads one "inside" to meet one's own demons, fears, resistance, terrors, and limitations, and to find the faith and inner power that says we are much more than our physical bodies. Many cultures past and present engage the fire in such a way of sacred ritual. I was a few months away from my forty-first birthday, a year that was a milestone in many ways, and one that I had wanted to honor all year long so that I could step into my future more fully, with more sacredness, and with more understanding of my purpose of being on this earth.

My state of being totally shifted during this ritual until I was standing in front of the fire facing the rising full moon as it slid above the mountains directly in my vision. I felt like I was not only stepping into the fire but putting my foot directly onto the moonbeams that they might carry me up into the magic of my expanded self. I walked not quickly as I had been instructed (I simply forgot everything that had been said), but slowly and deliberately, as if a force who knew much more than I had taken over. The instructions, the leader, and the other participants were only vague memories in the moment. I stood alone at the sacred juncture of my past and my future, in the moment of now.

As I made my way out of the fire to rejoin the circle of fellow travelers, I was left with the feeling that this expanded state of awareness was my true home and place of residence. I was also left with a scorched left foot in three places that swelled to unbelievable proportions over the next few hours and days. My right foot which had spent just as much time in the hot coals was completely free from injury. The pain of my left foot was not to be denied, though, and my awareness shifted from that pain, to the lack of injury to the other foot, to asking for the meaning, and back to the feeling that the altered state of being was my natural home. Around and around my mind went.

It didn't make any sense to me that only one side was affected; I felt there must be a deeper reason why I was so vulnerable on my left side. I had ascribed to my left side the role of the feminine, so I simply sat with the question of what had allowed for such visible trauma to manifest to this part of my body. My dreams began to be very vivid, their intensity and messages more concrete. Clues began to appear. A few weeks before my birthday, I moved through a huge barrier into a place of memory, memory of sexual abuse as a young child by a close relative. It was shocking to my whole system, physically, emotionally, and mentally. I could not believe or understand how I could have repressed something so intense and harming for so many years. It made no sense, and yet my whole body and soul cried out in relief that at last the truth was known, if only to myself. I was surrounded by the incredible support of family and friends as I began to share it little by little, and it was then that I entered therapy, a long road to recovery, and a deeper faith that life does, indeed, give us just what we need when we need it, when we are ready to cope with it.

My entire focus shifted from a peripheral faith in God to a profound and enduring relationship in which my whole life is seeking to live in that place of magnetic faith. Ironically, after believing that no matter how grateful I was to the fire for the recovery of a huge part of my soul, I would never have the courage to endure the test again, I did actually face the fire once again on that very New Year's Eve. This time I discovered my joy and my undiluted power as I walked not once but twice across those hot, sacred coals into the next year and my future.

I have incredible gratitude to the Spirit of the Fire for having taken such time to bestow its grace and blessings upon me. I certainly don't advise this avenue for all people, but I have found in my life that the fire has been my ally, my friend, and my teacher through such things as the firewalk, many sacred sweat lodges, and hot steamy hidden pools both in the southwestern United States and the high Tibetan mountain ranges. I have met my strength and joined hands with God to walk through terrifying but powerful inner darkness.

Fire is a wonderful analogy, as is reflected in the following journaling by a colleague who combines midwifery and motherhood in a way that speaks of the purity of integration.

The reality is that writing about what midwifery means to me would itself be a book, a book about life, in fact, that I

might pursue during a less intense time in my life. Writing about what midwifery means to me involves some quiet time for reflection and thoughtful consideration which I have very little of these days. Here's what I have to share. Nothing profound, nothing inspirational, just a little reality from my present life. With a touch of editing, here's a recent excerpt from my journal. . . .

It's been said that a laboring woman must go down into the depths of hell to bring forth her babies, to walk through the fire, to face the Death Crone eye to eye, and then, completely humbled, birth life anew.

I have seen in the women I attend, that they must completely release control, some would say, "totally lose it" before they can give birth. This is something of profound importance. It's frequently vocal or verbal, though I've seen it in the physical through gesture, posture or expression.

As midwife, I am there to let her go, off to that place all alone, and I am there to welcome her return, forever changed.

As mother to my children, I find that this trip through the fire happens again and again, long since the times of their births. Though not perhaps to the dramatic depths as in birthing, it's a difficult and painful trip just the same. I wish someone would have told me. The mothers I know don't share about this easily.

As my children test the limits in their lives, most of which I must define at this young time, I find that when I "lose it" they will relent. And you can't fake "losing it." You truly have to go there, to the darkness, the ugliness, the insanity, to return humbled, perhaps even ashamed.

It's like there's this dangerous high cliff out there that I'm responsible for protecting them from, but in order for them to truly see it, I must go over. It's like being pushed into the fire, but without a midwife to help me see that it's where I must go, it's where all mothers go. Without a midwife to welcome me back.

Journal entry April 1997

Chapter Eleven
Midwifery As Grace

As one goes through Life experiencing new Horizons, every once in awhile, he finds an oasis where the atmosphere is pleasant and goodness abounds. Our birth experience both prenatally and in labor was one of those oases—the kindness of everyone we will cherish forever.

A new dad's response

I feel so blessed to have had your friendship, support, guidance and wisdom to help me bring forth my children. It is truly a gift to have had you always holding the space for me, trusting me and trusting in the process. I can't tell you how grateful I am for that.

A mom's letter

We want to thank you for helping us bring our child into this world with the highest consciousness and intention and beauty possible. You helped us, as a couple, to be empowered under divinely nurturing conditions. . . . Thank you for honoring us.

From a parent's note

Thank you for reminding me of my inner strength when I needed it most.
A young mother's thank-you note

Happy Mommy's Day to the woman who helped make it possible for me to <u>be</u> a mommy!
A friend's kind words

So, in the final analysis, what do I know about being a midwife? It is challenging. It is rewarding. It is a blessing. It is demanding. It requires commitment, integrity, courage, fearlessness, surrender. It builds strength, patience, faith, trust, and endurance. It develops the ability to focus and to experience the joys, trials, and triumphs that life has to offer. It opens one's life to receiving grace. It invites the angels into one's awareness.

Being a midwife is about creating a container of safety and loving and equanimity that is big enough to allow another the room to explore, to grow, to encounter the unknown, and to emerge as a woman transformed by life. A midwife is challenged to move beyond judgments, opinions, thoughts, and personal agendas each and every moment. This is not because she needs to be perfect and be beyond her humanness but because she has learned the value of stepping aside, if only for brief moments of time, to truly see the magnificence and perfection of another soul and its particular way of being in the world. It becomes the way of the midwife to nurture and support and call the beauty of another into being, to recognize sometimes even before those we support the perfection that exists within.

A midwife holds life in reverence and respect. She learns to honor the life-giving force no matter what name she might personally give to it, and to protect it as one would a tiny ember until it can burst forth into flame on its own. A midwife becomes the witness to the flow of life, to the flow of Grace. Being a midwife is a great blessing in so much as it is an opportunity to be blessed and to share those blessings with others during such profound and intimate times.

Every midwife I know has a unique and special way of "being" with women, with their families and friends, with themselves. But to greater or lesser degrees, they each embody that spirit of life that calls them forth into service, serving to the best of their abilities all those in need. It is a path that offers true transcendence of so many aspects of our individual ego parts.

Midwife literally means "with woman," and for many years, I translated that into meaning I had to do something, to play an active, leading role in this event called birth. It was based to some degree on fear, fear that I wasn't good enough unless I "did" enough. I felt unworthy of being called a human being unless I could prove how much I knew, how valuable and necessary I was to people's lives. That I looked often to these women, to these births, for the reflection of my own worth, my own goodness, is a sad state of affairs, but it has been painfully true over the years. Call it co-dependence; call it dysfunctional; call it my inheritance and my legacy from the women in my family, following a long, painful tradition.

Gradually, with grace and many years of time, I began to recognize that my focus outside myself gave me nothing permanent, nothing nourishing, nothing but a momentary sense of worthiness, and I felt the exhaustion of that way of living each day of my life. I began to pray to be shown a way out of this dilemma. And I found that the way out was IN! I began to focus on my inner world, on that aspect of my being that held the truth, that held the sacred, divine part of my soul. I was determined to find out the truth of who I am, and to tap even greater strength and courage within myself to continue the journey.

I noticed, gradually at first but with a gathering of momentum, that I had become more aware of a power that came through me and effected changes. It was a power that I was not identified with nor attached to that allowed me to separate myself from outcomes or how it might look from the outside. I could actually feel and sometimes see in a shimmer of light that very force that was working through me. In these times, I was blessed just as much as was the recipient of my ministrations. There were still painful moments, there still are painful moments, when I am aware of this power that I call God working through me alone with the awareness of that sometimes-subtle and sometimes-not-so-subtle desire for recognition, for acknowledgement, for being seen. It is a place of feeling like I can never be enough or do enough to justify my existence.

I am challenged in these moments to recognize the wounded and vulnerable place that lives inside me and to comfort and support myself as a parent to a small child, without trying to manipulate or control my world to have this need met. I am becoming more able to look for the reflections that are genuine and authentic, and to also look to myself and to a Higher Source for support and encouragement for the steps I am taking. I am learning to become my own midwife in the midst of my own birthing and dying pains—the birth of the new and the dying away of the old, outmoded forms of behavior, thought, and reaction.

One birth that I remember most vividly brought the lesson home to me in a gentle, loving way that we are each and every one of us enough simply by our presence. We don't have to be anything more than what we already are in this very moment. This woman had two young, beautiful children whose beauty went far beyond their physical appearance. They were bright, loving, and full of life, veritable little light beams. Sheryl loved them totally and was able to be with them in a way that nourished their growth magnificently. I would watch them interact as she was "mother" to them, setting appropriate boundaries in a loving and respectful way. Waves of pain would wash over me as I remembered my own mothering skills which seemed so shallow in contrast.

Over time, I began to confide in her about the pain I was feeling after our visits. I respected her and felt very close to her, and yet I would spend days after our visits feeling incredible remorse about my past as both a parent and a daughter. I could feel the rigidity of my responses both as a child and as a mother. It was a really profound place of suffering. Sheryl listened but didn't say much, although I could feel that she was with me in a way that was respectful and caring, not judging or condemning. More time passed and we began to develop a deeper relationship that went beyond the immediate experience of her pregnancy.

I anticipated her birth with excitement, like it was someone in my own family. Her labor caught me by surprise. It was much longer than her others and much harder, in her perspective. I spend a great deal of time supporting her during contractions, supporting her husband as he sought to comfort and support her, and interacting with the kids who came and went during the long day-turned-night labor. I held her hand, rubbed her back, spoke words of encouragement, gave suggestions, and gently guided her into changing positions when she did not truly want to do it. And I loved her. Somehow she was the sister I never had. I kept calling a fellow midwife just to make sure I wasn't missing anything or losing my perspective.

With a suddenness that was actually shocking, the baby rotated and was born in only a few pushes. I think the truth was that I didn't have time to jump into my "professional" position at the birth. I was still loving her and walking through this labor one step at a time. As I held this beautiful baby girl, I realized that this birth was a huge blessing. I had stepped *beyond the normal boundaries of midwife to be absolutely and positively* present from my heart. And as this little baby had slid into my welcoming hands, I had heard the flutter of angels' wings surrounding each of us, as a melody that spoke of the profound miracle of birth echoed throughout the room. Was this my imagination? Was it a dream? Or was it the grace-bestowing gift of God? I can never answer from a scientific perspective; I can only answer from my heart and know how it touched my soul and eased a burden of pain from my shoulders and filled my heart with light and joyfulness.

Sheryl in her infinite wisdom validated my experience, as it had touched her in a place she had now remembered from childhood.

> *I felt myself suddenly surrender in those last moments knowing there was nowhere else to go, nothing more that I could do. I seemed to fall into and then away from the pain and I was left in a deep stillness that shimmered like the morning dew. I felt the pain and the fear and the tiredness fall away in those precious moments. And I was suddenly four years old sitting up in the hayloft with my feet swinging off the side of the open door while my mother sat beside me. We were watching the sun setting in the distance and I could hear the sounds of the sparrows in the trees nearby. My dad was walking towards us from the field. It was one of those moments in time that became timeless. I knew that life was perfect no matter what might happen in this world of ours. I saw you sitting there beside me and you were my mother. . . . I knew and trusted and could let go into your hands because they were hands that loved me.*
> . . .

She cried and cried; she touched my core. I felt like I was being offered a healing if I could reach out and take it inside me. She wasn't asking me to do anything, to be any different than I was, to make anything happen or to know anything else. I could simply be "me" in those moments of honesty, connection, and truth. And I knew that I must come to a place that could forgive myself and acknowledge my humanity and not be afraid to continue to reach out, even when I was my most "human" in making mistakes or "doing it wrong."

To take the feeling of unworthiness that I talked of earlier a step further, I have had the experience during this time in Nepal of what may be the root cause of my ignorance that has kept the cycle of suffering going. In varying situations, I have found myself while in a state of grief uttering the words, *"I only have my heart to give and I'm afraid it isn't enough."* And I am reminded that many great Masters have stated over and over again that the heart is the only thing, in fact, that we have to give. So, it seems as if I am being gently led back to the beginning, where altruism and compassion are pure and true. In this purity, I can touch into my own genuine, loving, open heart. It seems that the giving that comes from this place is truly healing for both the giver and the receiver, while anything other than this is often based on confusion and delusion.

One incredibly special birth that taught me of this was with the daughter of a close friend, who was the daughter-in-law of another close friend. I had known her as a young high school girl and watched her grow into womanhood in a powerful and delightful way. She was strong and courageous in her roles of wife, mother, woman, and daughter. She let no stone be unturned in her quest for truth and healing. Having her second child at home was an experience that brought us closer and into a more mutually rewarding exchange. We sought the ground to have our own relationship, no longer content to keep the distance that the previous roles had assigned us. She had to make hard decisions during this pregnancy due to some complications. She struggled, she wept. She pleaded and cried. And she did just what was asked of her in spite of it all. It was truly a time of healing, showing her great strength and courage as much to herself as to the others in her life.

Her birth was intense and fast. The memory that will forever stay with me is sitting on the couch looking into her eyes as she let the waves of contractions wash over her. The room and everyone else in it disappeared and we were left alone, two souls, one loving and supporting and the other meeting the magic and mystery of life in all its elemental force. It was powerful beyond words. There was an exchange of energy that was not about words or anything of this world, actually. It moved both of us from one place in our personal histories to another, a step towards something greater on our paths, individually and collectively. No matter what happens in our lives, there will always be this moment to fall back upon where the truth was revealed for but a moment. That was all it took.

It is during these times, when I forget that I am supposed to "remember to remember who I am," that I must give pause to the cycle of thoughts in my mind. I remind myself that I have had just as many experiences of having an open heart as I have had of thinking myself so limited. There are countless images I hold in my mind of handing a baby into a mom's waiting arms, of offering silent support during a time of grief and loss with a touching of hands, of guiding a dad's hands as their child is born with his assistance, of precious moments filled with laughter where there is no need for words, and of tears rolling down my cheeks in response to a long-distance call by a new parent to tell the "news" to waiting family across the country. Beautiful images float in and out of the tender looks that pass between a couple, of the exhilaration of a job well done, of celebration as a sibling is brought in to touch the new baby, and of tired, aching bodies that reach out to embrace and welcome the tiny being. Each and every moment of joining in this unique and special time is the true gift for my heart, the true gift from my heart.

Patricia and her amazing family taught me early in my time of attending home births about the magic and mystery, love and bonding, celebration and joy that arise from our connections with each other, family and friends alike. Her first labor began on Christmas night, gentle waves of contractions that increased steadily in intensity throughout the night into the next day. I watched as her family poured into her home, spelling each other, walking beside her, sitting with her, talking to her, supporting her as she made forays out into the cold winter's day in an effort to speed up the process. Minutes turned into hours and hours turned into another full day. I called for support from my partner midwife as Patricia's family and friends continued their vigil at her side.

I will never forget the sounds of celebration when finally this precious baby made its entrance into the welcoming arms of those who had stood at her side. It wasn't until it was over, and I had retreated to the other room to sip hot tea and watch the flickering of Christmas tree lights as they made dancing shadows upon the walls, that I realized what a gift I had just been given, what a blessing it had been to participate in this event. The truest meaning of Christmas had been revealed in the love and magic that I had witnessed being bestowed from one to another. I went back to their home three days in a row to bask in the glory of the incredible love that had filled that house and welcomed that new family in their journey together. It was an experience of being truly immersed in the teachings of sacred loving and deep bonding between people who cared about each other from such a pure place inside themselves. These moments come back to me at odd times, but never do they fail to appear during the holiday season when lights flicker and the cold air penetrates my awareness. It was truly Grace manifesting.

At the old people's home, there is a young handicapped boy with cerebral palsy who I go feed at lunchtime. His name is Rajis, and what I experience in his presence as he laughs and claps excitedly at my approach is nothing but love and delight for his existence, for his beingness, for the preciousness of his life, and for the sheer pleasure that his life touches mine. His life matters to me, matters deeply. I offer an hour of my time, but more important, I offer him my attention, my respect, and my unconditional love. It's not difficult to do. And, I wonder, am I giving it from my own depths of love and compassion, or is he, by his purity and lack of guile, drawing that state from the depths of my being so that I am aware of it, so that I can reach into it, and so that he can bask in it?

It is definitely a synchronistic event as far as I can understand at this point, a coming together for the enrichment of both of our souls. That we cannot speak each other's language is irrelevant. What we exchange is far greater than words could ever convey anyway. I am moved to tears simply by remembering his place in my life for this period of time.

As I review the past twenty-seven years and think about all the people and situations I have encountered in my career, I begin to wonder why those particular people or those particular circumstances? What did I learn? What did I overlook? What did I resist learning or seeing? What was I exposed to that I needed at that very moment? What was it about that event that changed my perspectives of myself or life or birth, or gave me the opportunity to glimpse the greater force of God? What were the projections that either I was putting onto someone else or someone else was putting onto me? Where did I fight to hold onto old ways of being and where did I step forward into the unknown in a way that forever changed my life? I imagine how a drop of water dripping over stone gradually, over eons of time, can change the course of a river, how it polishes the stone and creates beautiful new landscapes. It is as if each and every event, encounter, and moment, whether I found it pleasant or unpleasant, and full of praise or blame, joy or sadness, has had the same sort of effects on the being I call "me." I, as a midwife and a human being, am a sculpture in progress, just as we all are.

In speaking of midwifery as grace, I am reminded that it is not all glory, all joy, or all giving. There is a dark side that cannot be denied in our culture. And this dark side comes out of our judicial system. While there are multi-layered issues at stake in medical malpractice that need to be addressed, I choose not to attempt to define those issues here. What I do want to address is the impact on women who have chosen this life path of midwifery or the healing profession in general. Here is the story of one midwife who has walked this path in the not-too-distant past.

Looking back, when I first decided to be a midwife, I had romantic thoughts about what it was going to be like. I imagined a softly lit room, a beautiful birth with a couple I was connected to, and me going home and crawling into bed at peace with the world and my contribution to it as I basked in the magic of the experience. Midwifery school was very difficult, and sometimes I questioned my decision, but these visions helped carry me through.

And so in September 1991, I packed my belongings and moved to a new city away from my friends and family to begin a new career. Just me and my dog. It was a new life and I was so excited to be starting this adventure, I had this cool job "catching babies" and sharing the most important time in a woman's life. I was so lucky! The first few months were everything I could have hoped for. I loved my job. It was busy and fun and bright and magic. I loved the responsibility and the learning of new skills. The connection with the patients was different than I had thought, but every bit as fulfilling. I was making good friends and exploring a different part of the country.

In January 1992, I attended a birth that was difficult. I called my consultant and he ended up doing a forceps delivery. It wasn't any different from any of the hundreds of other forceps deliveries I had seen as a nurse. But I felt the responsibility differently. But it came with the territory, it was part of what I had signed up for. I unfortunately didn't understand fully what that meant. I kept loving my job until the following October 1992, when risk management called regarding a case. This was the beginning of the end of my innocence. It started with risk management saying "we don't think you'll lose your job" and my stunned surprise that that could even be a possibility.

My deposition was in December 1992. I remember not wanting to tell anyone, not even or especially my family. I was embarrassed like I was to blame. But I knew we had done nothing wrong. The deposition was awful. I totally lost it in the middle of it and was crying in the bathroom with my attorney. Then we waited. Except for occasional brief flares, there was little that appeared to happen for years. Finally, in July of 1995, we went to trial for the first time. It was a horrible experience and it ended in a hung jury! To have to sit in the courtroom while an attorney talks about how uncaring you are, and how you intentionally hurt this baby, and how unethical you are is like torture. The second trial was set to go in January of 1996. The day it was due to begin, they settled. It was almost anticlimactic, but at least it was over.

Somewhere in the whole experience, you lose sight of why you are here. And you begin to not trust them. "They" are the ones you wanted to connect with and help and share the magic with. The betrayal cuts very deep. All your decisions are colored, the information you give is affected, the way you care is guarded. You can't get too involved cause it is too scary. Then it isn't just the patients but your colleagues as well. They might think you are too paranoid or overreacting. But if they haven't walked in those shoes they can't know how it feels to sit with an attorney defending why you said or didn't say something. And it hurts that they don't or can't understand. It is a very lonely place.

But I sat with it and moved through it. And it changed me. I lost my innocence and I grew up fast. Midwifery doesn't "fill me" like it does others. I like my job (most days) and I do know that it is a cool job. It keeps me busy and I do meet nice people, some of whom I connect with. I am selective about who and how much I give myself. And every so often I have an incredibly, truly profound moment of magic. They don't come often, but that is more than most people can say about their jobs.

She speaks for most of us who call midwifery their path when she talks of the "truly profound moment of magic" as the reason she keeps doing what she has been trained to do. The heart of the midwife is genuinely caring and committed and resourceful throughout the good times and the difficult times. We may not like to think of the possibility of encountering situations that put us in legal jeopardy, but they are, nevertheless, a part of our working environment. And when we do face these situations, we are forced to look deeply within at why we want to be with women during pregnancy and birth. We are forced to look at how competent and knowledgeable we feel about this path. We are forced to look at how dedicated we can be in the face of this certain trauma of being accused and potentially found at fault, and decide whether the benefits and rewards, emotionally and spiritually and financially, are offset by the risks. We come face to face with looking at our deepest beliefs and basic intentions. There is only one way to go and that is through the fire. And, as the midwife in the above story shared, we cannot help but be changed. We do in some indefinable way "lose our innocence," and our ability to trust in quite the same way is shattered to a greater or lesser degree.

I have had to answer these questions for myself in a time that was difficult to do rationally. I can only reaffirm my commitment to providing safe and supportive care to women and their babies, knowing in my heart that I went into midwifery because I cared and because I believed I could create an environment that honored and respected women and children and their families. It is my path of service no matter what the consequences or outcomes. As midwives, we are challenged to face the fear and the pain, recognize the value, and come to know our purity of heart in providing these kinds of services to women and babies.

Ram Dass and Paul Gorman in *How Can I Help?,* speak about this pain, about opening to it and discovering the possibility of freedom within it.

> *As we play the edge of our pain—gently opening, acknowledging, and allowing—the suffering it has caused diminishes. If we further dissolve the boundaries, letting ourselves enter into the pain and the pain enter into us, we can see the possibility of going beyond it to where the heart is freer. We've never been so vulnerable, so defenseless, and yet somehow so safe. The surrender we were so frightened of turns out to be not defeat but a kind of victory. . . . As our understanding of our suffering deepens, we become available at deeper levels to those we would care for.*

It is for these reasons that I call this my purpose; my path; and my call to know myself, the truth, and God as I am midwife to another and to myself. It is the incredible opportunity to meet myself, to meet another, to greet myself, and to greet another, as I find myself truly with women at such a time that fosters authenticity, spontaneity, truth, wisdom, and compassion.

Birth takes us past the barriers of our culture to reveal the essence and all that stands in the way of our genuineness. I am touched to the core of my being by our mutual vulnerability; our depth of need for human support, contact, and love; and our greater capacity to reach out into the part of ourselves that we usually keep silenced or hidden or devalued.

Birth is not the end. Birth is only the beginning. What it is an end to are our illusions of our smallness, our beliefs in our inability to bring forth something sacred and new, our beliefs that we are limited, and bound by the laws of man to stay limited. Birth teaches us about our greatness, our vastness, our creativity, and our ability to encounter and embrace something we cannot truly name, something at once illusive and yet more real than our everyday minds, our conditioning, our bodies. It is our true nature, and we see it reflected in the eyes of our children, in the eyes of our loved ones, in the eyes of our critics even, and in the mirrors of our own souls if only for brief and fleeting timeless moments.

This sense of purpose calls me from behind the name of midwife, as well as from the experience of being a midwife. I believe that it calls from behind each and every job or kind of work that we do. I listen to the silence that is behind the sounds of my everyday world, and I hear the call to trust, to sit quietly in that inner place of the heart, to listen to those around me, and to remain witness to all that unfolds within my being and my life. Is it always easy to do? Of course not. But I know that that call is for life, for birth, and for the emergence and the renewal of the force that acts behind and within our individual lives.

Harmony is the word that comes to mind as I feel the flow of this awareness within me. Words from Jean Shinoda Bolen in *Close to the Bone* describe this state succinctly.

> *Harmony is being on the right path, being one with it— making a living doing work that is absorbing and consistent with your personal values, doing what you have a gift for. ... Harmony is uninhibited, unselfconscious spontaneity, the immediacy of laughter, the welling up of*

tears. Harmony happens when behavior and belief come together, when inner archetypal life and out life are expressions of each other, and we are being true to who we are.

Life is precious. Life is an opportunity. Life is an expression of the Divine. Let us hold life as we hold a precious, innocent baby and live a sacred life as we were intended, midwife to each other and to the deeper, innate truthfulness that lives inside each one of us. May we be filled with grace as we each seek greater and deeper understanding of what our lives mean to us in this oh-so-brief time we walk upon this earth.

Om shanti. May peace prevail.

Chapter Twelve
Coming Full Circle

You took my hand and walked beside me as I began a journey into the greater part of myself. You believed in me when I doubted. You nurtured me when I fell down and did not want to get up again. You shouted words of encouragement when nameless fears overtook me. You held a greater image of me than I could have ever possibly envisioned on my own at the time. You challenged me when I thought I already knew, and made me grow and see things from a different perspective. You taught me how to reach out and really see another, and how to connect that seeing with an intuitive awareness of what was needed in the moment. You taught me to trust my intuition when I was afraid of being wrong. You stood by me when I made mistakes. You loved me even when I didn't love myself. You never gave up your faith in my ability to become more. Words can never repay you for the path you revealed that led me down steep steps into the depths of the well of my soul where I found the road Home. Thank you from the bottom of my heart.

I came to this point in the path through numerous and varied experiences, through being touched by countless people, and through the support of truly caring people in both my work environment and my personal life. The words above are written to the people who have impacted my life in deep and dramatic ways, including physicians, friends, co-workers, and the special God-friends who walk the spiritual path alongside me. Each of these people has nourished and nurtured me in different ways, at different times, in different circumstances, and for different reasons. No less than the deepest honor and respect can I offer to each of them. They have helped shape what my life is today and have supported this journey of midwifery with their abiding faith in Life itself.

As I have contemplated the ending of this writing, I have come to see that life is definitely a process that continues into the next moment, one after the other after the other. I could, honestly, be writing this for the rest of my life, since there is never an end to the teachings, the realizations and the new beginnings. Midwifery never ends even as the years pass and we can no longer give birth in the physical sense ourselves or we choose not to deliver babies any longer. Life is a process that continually calls on the birthing of some new aspect of our being. We are called forth into our own greatness by something bigger than our small, limited selves.

I recently spoke with a woman who is very sensitive to the various levels of our awareness and to the importance, as she perceives it, of events in our lives. She shared the following story with me.

She recently attended the funeral of the physician who had delivered her mother of a daughter, this woman being that daughter. This physician had been a family doctor and had seen her through the first seven years of her life. As she had entered into this final celebration of his life and life's work, she was overcome with the profound sense of safety and connection that he had given her as a tiny baby and young child. She shared with me what she believed to be the profound gift and importance of this bond that goes throughout life with us.

I was moved to tears at her words as I also made a deeper commitment once again to be as conscious as I possibly could at each and every birth I am privileged to take part in.

This brings me to questions about the rest of my life. Where am I now and where am I going? They are difficult questions to answer and yet the underlying themes speak of grace. I am coming to see that my work is actually only beginning. I have accomplished the things that my culture has said are important; I have had the marriage, the children, the career, the house, the car, the travel, and the recognition. My work might seem to be finished, in one sense. But I am catching a glimpse of something magical afoot, as the years of wisdom and love come together to forge a container that is so large and strong that I can give more of myself than I ever thought possible. That container is God-given and God-nourished and can never run dry. It is the gift of hard work and a life full of challenges and pain and disappointment and heartache. It is the gift of life in its fullness and life in its joyfulness, connection, caring, and commitment.

We don't have a lot of older women to emulate as we walk into the later years, although there are more and more stepping forward to dream the dreams of our future as a united and peaceful people on this planet. I want to be one of those. I want to take my strength and my courage, my desire to experience the adventures of life, my patience, and my faith into the arena of the next half of my life, or however long is left for me to walk with God upon this earth. I want to be able to dig deeply into the essence of my soul and pull forth these qualities that I have spoken of as I journey Home to God, remembering to remember who I am, where I came from, and where I am going. I want to blaze my own trail which speaks of surrendering to God's will and not my own. I want to blaze that trail upon the larger already-worn path of the masters and seers of time past and follow them home. I seek that path and yet I know that I can do nothing but follow and trust this path itself. The path IS the goal.

Shortly before finishing this, I was faced with the profound realization of how short this life is and how great an opportunity we have to live it according to our highest principles. A dear friend and colleague was diagnosed with cancer and gave birth to twins all in the same week. My heart was wrenched with deep sadness and grief as I contemplated the meaning of life, of giving birth and of dying. I faced my own mortality with a huge question in my heart of what my life specifically was all about.

In the first days after her diagnosis, I willingly would have given my life for her so that she could be with her new family for many, many years. My life seemed so full and complete; hers seemed to be just beginning. As I sat with these feelings, I began to see that the life God has given me must mean little to me if I could give it away so easily. That is not to deny the purity of my initial response of wanting to exchange my life for hers. There was something genuine and loving in that wish. But in pondering what I thought I had left to offer or accomplish, or how it seemed that I had nothing left to give, I realized that I still have much to learn about the value of a human life. It became clear in my meditations that we as human inhabitants need people to live in a way that honors life from beginning to end, to strive for the union with the Divine, and to live our lives with dignity and honor, touching and sharing the path as we forge ahead into the unknown, the unplanned, and the unexpected.

Jean Shinoda Bolen, again in the book *Close to the Bone*, talks of this path of the midwife in a different way.

At the end of life as at its beginning, a woman may act as midwife, only this time as midwife to the soul as it crosses the threshold. Held in the arms of a woman, or more rarely by a man whose interior feminine allows him access to the mother archetype, a dying person may feel himself or herself held by the Mother, embraced by the energy that surrounds both, participating in a prayer without words, receiving unconditional love through the body of the woman as the conduit.

Her final gift to me was the awareness of my own unique path and my vulnerability that urges me to open my heart even wider in the midst of great pain and loss, surrendering more of my smaller, limited self to what I truly am. Her life touched mine so deeply, and even though she no longer walks the human path beside me, she has nonetheless left her mark, and I can feel her gentle urging to "let go and let God." It has become for me not giving up and simply existing in my known world. It is about becoming a midwife to that part of me that seeks to blossom, to merge and emerge, to grow and become and give to those in my world whether I know them or not. Living in this manner speaks so much of faith, with a strength born out of this faith. Wayne Muller in *Legacy of the Heart* tells of this place poignantly.

This quiet, intimate place of hidden strength is the place where God lives within us, where what is eternal and trustworthy has been our private ally and companion. When we live our lives by acting out of this deep place of knowing, when we listen to the voices that speak to us from this inner place of knowing, when we listen to the voices that speak to us from this inner place of sanctuary, then we may truly begin the practice of faith.

So, I end where I began, welcoming the call to adventure as I step into my future in a way that honors my own path and the paths of all those who share this journey. May all that I have learned from the women in my life continue to nurture and nourish this part of me that seeks expression and expansion. May my sadhana deepen as the truth penetrates more completely and may it continue to shape and reshape my life as I walk this sacred path.

May you take anything that you might have learned from these women with you as you continue your own unique and sacred journey. With the greatest of blessings, I wish you a safe and happy crossing.

Printed in the United States
214056BV00001B/2/A

9 781932 047073